D0631468

Unspoken Feelings
Of a Gentleman
II

Inspired by:

You

Written by:

Me

Copyright © 2016 by Pierre Alex Jeanty

All rights reserved. No part of this publication may be reproduced, stored in a retrieval system, or transmitted in any form or by any means- electronic, mechanical, photocopying, recording, or otherwise—without the written permission of the publisher.

Jeanius Publishing LLC

PO Box 1562

Lehigh Acres, FL 33970

For more information, please visit:

jeaniuspublishing.com; or

gentlemenhood.com

Cover Design: Jaime Hernandez

Editors: Dana Ezell Jackson, Carla DuPont Huger

Illustration: Tremanda Pewett

ISBN-13: 978-0-9862556-7-0

Other books
By Pierre Alex Jeanty:

Unspoken Feelings of a Gentleman

To The Women I Once Loved

Dedication

To You, the Readers,

You motivate me to continue, not only to share my writing with you, but my life, sacrificing personal parts of myself for your growth. Without your eyes and your investment, this wouldn't be possible. Thank you!

To My Wife,

You push me to be a better man every single day. You push me to keep taking this as far as possible. I can't stop thanking you. I love you.

Unspoken Feelings
Of a Gentleman
II

CONTENTS

Introduction

Becoming a man isn't an easy journey. Like everything else in life, it has its challenges and is full of adventures. In today's generation, it is not the easiest thing to be a man. When you are indeed trying to become, '*A Man*', rather than trying to be, '*The Man*', fitting in is often easier than standing out. Although standing out is being yourself and staying true to yourself, it requires going against the norm and what society teaches. To be a man, is to be a fish swimming in the opposite direction of the other fish; unfortunate but true.

Quite a lot of males find comfort in being less than a man, despite how long they've lived. They grow up, but never mature. Their age goes up, while they remain stuck in immaturity. They continue looking at maturity as something of no value or as unnecessary. The current world we live in does not make it easy to turn away from being less than a man, it actually promotes it. More than ever, being immature and irresponsible is being applauded and it's actually entertaining to many. Despite how unsupportive the world may be to the man who is attempting to be the gentleman, he is needed in communities and this world. Choosing to 'Man' up may be a difficult task, but one that is quite fulfilling.

Far too many males in this world are growing up not knowing how to be a man and not knowing how to mature and transform into who God needs them to be on this earth. Many don't know how to be themselves. There is an identity crisis affecting both sexes, but more common in males. They just do not know how to love themselves nor have enough guidance to push towards being who they are designed to be in this world.

Manhood now is not only threatened by the terrible role models and false ideologies of manhood, but men are at war with themselves and society's fraudulent standards. They are also at war with women who want them to pay for the sins their fathers committed against their mothers. Revenge to some is being a better version of themselves, while to others it is returning the hurt to those who did them wrong.

Lots of women are seeking revenge; their idea of strong womanhood is overthrowing men. Although it appears to be harmless, it is causing quite a bit of damage. Women have had their share of bad times throughout history and believe that they are finally giving men a taste of their own medicine. However, a lot of men drinking 'their own medicine' aren't the ones who need to be healed from their evil ways.

Many men being wronged aren't villains. However, they become villains as a way to keep themselves from becoming victims. It is safe to say that we have been victims to society's demands, but are now being bullied. Almost everywhere you go online, you will find a quote floating around with the message that men aren't good enough. The underlying message is that their value is based on how good they are to a woman and how much they can please a woman.

I do believe that part of a woman's happiness is a reflection of the type of man she is with. I do *not* believe it is the man's job to make her happy and keep only her happy. Nor should the world revolve so much around what men should do to meet a woman's needs.

Lots of good men are hurting. Their fathers, homeboys and other men in their lives are doing the usual, telling them to grow up and be a man about it. All that really means is to act numb to the pain and go chase pleasure instead. On the other hand, women are saying that the men are receiving karma for having wronged them.

There are many things that we do not voice. Not only because men have been taught to shut up and treat hurt and emotional needs as if they aren't existent, but a lot of men believe that women don't want to hear about their deep thoughts. We, as men, do not see them as willing to view our scars as battle wounds while we evolve. Instead, we feel that when we open up, our vulnerability sometimes is used as a way to manipulate us. We are discouraged from being free and open by everyone.

Being a man has become a curse for many. Being a solid man of valor, who is faithful and of good character, seems to be a burdensome goal that results in no real gain. There are far too many characteristics lacking due to a generation suffering from moral decline. We cannot build men with the absence of good and positive examples, mentorship and leadership. Not enough males are transforming boys into men, passing on the wisdom they've gained.

Many young men are growing up without the guidance of a father, or a positive role model or guardian. Instead, they learn from what they see on the TV screen or the internet believing those things to be right. They easily fall victim to their own understanding. Subjective moral reasoning is becoming the thing to rely on when no one is there to teach them. Right and wrong is not primarily black and white these days, it's mostly in the gray area. The world tells males to man up, stand up, and be leaders. At the same time they are encouraged to be loving, caring, faithful, and open to love. Being human, there is no way to do it all. We are told to be good and great, but not instructed on how to get there. People simply suggest that we figure it out on our own and that we figure it out fast.

As males, we will never grow into the men we ought to be, unless we open our mouths and get honest with ourselves. It is often difficult for men to communicate sentimental things to each other, to partners, or even family members. This lack of communication creates a lot of internal issues that are not dealt with. Once again, no need to talk about it, just 'man up and let it go'.

We walk around as zombies, lifeless yet still trying to experience life. Mummies who cannot speak. Flesh, filled with bottled up emotions that are ready to explode. Those of us who do not fall victim to cancerous coaching about manhood and are able to become loving men who are open to love, tend to find it hard to pass down those attributes. It is difficult to teach our sons, nephews and boys in the community because men typically don't talk about such things. We cannot improve, if our hearts aren't poured, worries aren't voiced, and if pain is not dealt with. Then lessons aren't shared.

Men do not need to soften up in times like this, in a world full of people who are too sensitive with soft skin. They do need to be more in touch with their sensitive side without letting it dominate them. We practice too much of 'either/or'. There has to be a balance that includes 'and'. Too often as men, we try to hide our sensitive side by covering it up with a façade. As a man you should be: allowed to talk about heartbreaks, be allowed to cry, to love and mourn your pain, apologize and be apologized to, accept the consequences of your choices, but you should not fear vulnerability and let fears eat away at the good things in your life.

We (men) are human beings who go through things, need help, as well as love. However, we have grown to believe and have been required by society to feel we must be more than human. No one says this directly, but many show through their actions that they expect supernatural behavior from us. The balance that men need to have is sometimes hard to find. We are too quick to make our experiences our truth.

A man sometimes becomes closed and reacts coldly simply because a woman has failed to appreciate the loving and emotional side of him. When he did take a leap of faith to expose that side of him, he was made to feel like a fool for being nothing more than a human being craving love and affection.

There are times when a man can act in a way that people usually consider to be more feminine behavior; acting too soft hearted, emotionally weak, and whiny. These types of behaviors are far from the firm, manly expectation of what some women prefer. He may have softened because being a macho man instead of being a sensitive man was lacking in his previous relationship. Therefore, he became what that previous relationship needed, but over did it in the present relationship.

Life is about balance and we all need balance. It's too much of one or the other. We can only help ourselves if we allow people to see that we are human and when we stop believing that closed mouths and close hearts will magically get what us what we need. Healing is needed for so many men. A man cannot heal unless he leaves the door of his heart cracked open enough to let someone in; allowing those who care, the ones with the right medicine or bandages, who are truly willing to help him find the doctor (God) to heal him. He must also learn to love when someone makes the effort to slide in through the crack of his heart. He must be willing to open up more, to be more considerate, caring, and affectionate and an overall loving human being.

Having balance starts with understanding ourselves, understanding one another, knowing the deep things about one another, putting ourselves in each other's shoes. Understanding doesn't come without communication, without honesty, without conversations. *Unspoken Feelings* must be heard. It is through listening, that pain will be detected and when pain is detected healing can become the focus and be obtained.

These are the thoughts of a gentleman.

Not of a perfect man, but a gentleman.

These are thoughts of a man who once didn't see the freedom in 'freedom of speech'.

This is the journey of a man who is no different than any other man, yet who can relate to many men...

The *Residue*

If I Knew Better

I was not given a map of manhood,

I did not know which road to travel or which to ignore.

I had to find my way around and many times I drove in the wrong lane.

I could no longer wish for a map to this, but I did wish that someone would have handed me a bible a bit earlier,

I do not let the blame rest on my father for not being around to teach me better, but I do hold him accountable.

I messed up quite a few times and those times created a cycle.

A cycle of broken-hearted women, who became cold-hearted and cold to men who actually aimed to love them, and some of those men were on their way out the door of the good guy club and got the push they needed.

It hurts to know that I was a chef who contributed to the pot of brokenness in today's world.

Sometimes it hurts far more when you see women condemn you for your mistakes and older men call you a punk for your previous choices, when they had no interest in teaching you or those like you, any better.

How unfortunate,

The only help that I got was from people who needed just as much help as I.

I chased the virginity of young women, devaluing their precious temples, convincing some to share their hearts with me while introducing them to pain that can't be seen with the physical eye; I burned some with betrayal and clogged their brain with manipulation.

I have made quite a mess behind me,

I am forgiven because I met the savior, but I wonder if some of those women in my trail of bad choices are still laying where I left them, carrying their pain or if they met the savior as well and started on their own journey.

I do not yet have a daughter, but I watch my nieces grow and would fight any man who would wishes to harm them.

But I have hurt women in many ways.

The thing about growing and maturing is that you see where you failed and say, "Man I wish I knew better." You become happy about your progress, while staring at the fact that you didn't do better, stirring regret down to your bone marrow.

I do not make excuses for what I have done and I am divorced from that version of me, but I do wish I knew better.

If I would have known better, the population of broken women would be less, not by much, but less.

If I knew better, more women would believe in true love with less caution tape around their hearts and that would have helped more men. Less of them would have suffered from the wrath of those women.

If I knew better, I would not have caused so much pain to myself and would not have created so many scars, distorting my views about love and women.

If I knew better, I would have been a better man sooner, been a better husband and a better father.

But, I do not live in regret. Yet it's not easy to look at your past and realize the bad you contributed.

I do not make excuses for my past or my choices, but I live as someone who knows better, because now I do.

The thing about manhood is that it doesn't come with instructions. There are many men who have caused great pain to the opposite sex and continue to do so simply because they do not know better. It took me a while to realize the man who I was, doing wrong and meeting the wrong standards of society. It wasn't until I had caused enough damage, and when I finally had actual examples of real men involved in my life that I decided to start doing better.

In my younger days, when I lived a promiscuous lifestyle, I never once thought about my decisions and how they affected the ones I had been with. I never said to myself: "*Oh wow, this will hurt this girl bad, it's not fair to use this woman and break her heart.*" As I indulged in lust and my selfishness, nothing mattered but my own satisfaction. Those thoughts didn't travel anywhere near my brain.

I was ignorant and in my ignorance, I was applauded by other fools. I don't think enough people realize how much betrayal, heartbreak, manipulation, and emotional abuse can actually hurt people. A lot of people walk with scars from the past affecting their every move, causing them to make wrong choices and follow the wrong paths, without realizing that the pain and bitterness is the pilot of their lives. Many don't see how their experiences alter their perspective and can put them on a road full of fallacies, yet they believe it to be their truth.

Lots of people only know love to be what those who didn't love them taught them. There is a cycle of men hurting women and women hurting men and it exists mainly because not enough of us know better. Then there are some who know better but do not do better. I could not have enough hands to count how many times I've heard women tell me how their men are treating them poorly, yet those men do not see anything wrong with it. I also can't count how many times I have heard the cries of men who become victims of hurt women. While these men try to bring them happiness, women struggle to navigate the earth because they are in great fear, having their guards up and their walls beyond the heavens.

There are quite a good amount of women who get with immature men, who have yet to truly grow into their manhood, expecting them to be the man that they need. The women become disappointed, burying nothing but disappointment in their minds and false ideas of love and dating in their hearts. These women unknowingly pass over the good men, in effect doing the same thing that was done to them. It's really all some of them know, so the pain is all they offer, which their partner does not see until the relationship is past the honeymoon stage. A fair amount of people just are not ready for dating or choosing to learn from their relationships. A lot more men are not yet equipped for love, they have much more to learn that only experience can teach them, however the process is harmful to others. More than enough men are still learning from trial and error when it comes to love and more than enough women are facing the wrath of their errors.

This existing cycle has to stop; I do not blame men for it, but it truly starts with them. We are natural leaders, but unfortunately if we don't know where we are going, we as blind souls will lead women into ditches and holes. It's understandable that one will always be a work in progress and that people are always healing from something, but we cannot use the fact that we are still growing as a way to justify our wrongs. Enough of our women need restoration or are on the path to it. I do not think we can ever totally put an end to this vicious cycle, but I do believe it can be weakened. It all starts by teaching our young men and raising our boys correctly. If those who know better did their best to teach the next generation to be better, living better as example to those who need better, we would be further along.

This current generation is often referred to as a generation that is empty of morals, but it's because many have never been taught. There just aren't that many good role models to look up to, too many corrupt leaders and so forth. Numerous people from the generation before are simply looking at this generation and pointing fingers, without enough of them offering help. We must teach better, learn better, know better, do better, and be better so we can offer better.

My Dear Sisters,

An apology this is not, nor is it an excuse for the behaviors of my brothers. We have committed terrible crimes against you, some because of the bad condition of our hearts and others simply because we do not know better. I can never write off men's terrible choices, but the reality is that some of us do not know how to do better. Sometimes it takes us breaking enough hearts to finally lose something good and getting our own hearts broken to realize how wrong we are.

Believe it or not, some men's first heartbreak is them breaking the heart of a woman who they truly cared for. Until we taste our own medicine or see the capacity of our foolish choices, many of us will not change. This takes longer to happen for far too many men. You must leave until he does better; you do not have to endure the worst or be the perfect subject for his trial and error.

Women tend to end up with a man who has recently grown out of that, but you don't have to be the practice dummy who prepares that man for other women. Refuse to deal with nothing less than a man who has matured past the foolish doctrines of manhood.

The solution to end this cycle is a two-way street. It takes teaching men before they create a bath of destruction, but it also takes women not voluntarily becoming victims, surviving on false hope. I am not encouraging ladies to abandon the man who recognizes his mistakes and who is making strides to no longer be a man who ignorantly hurt them. But, I am telling you all to run from a relationship that is not only unhealthy, but that will never grow healthier. I am not saying to give up easily, I am simply encouraging you to stop holding on when it's not only hurting your hands, but every part of you.

Sincerely,

A Gentleman

Dreams

I had dreams, so did you.

I cannot tell you if it was because our visions could not see eye to eye or if our relationship wasn't meant to be, but I can tell you it was hell trying to build something that I was passionate about, while the only person by my side turned their back on me.

Everyone laughed at my thirst for the extraordinary and told me the ordinary is what I was born for; you did too.

Everyone found it to be silly when I said I would build my own brand and be an entrepreneur. They told me with laughter in their voice to keep my day job, to wake up every day and do what everyone else does, to take care of my responsibilities. Sadly, you did too.

They watched me put in effort, consistency and hard work instead of commending me. They said that I was wasting my time, you did too.

Out of everyone, you saw the sleepless nights, you knew about the times I hid in the restroom at my job to write. You were right there when carpal tunnel kidnapped my hands, limiting my writing. You saw the sweat and the tears and the struggle, everything from the inside, yet you acted like everyone else who was looking from the outside.

You couldn't support my dreams, so our relationship became a nightmare.

I felt alone, trying to fill in the space I have in my room for improvement.

I closed the door on you. I became closed. Closed to your opinions, your presence, closed to any support you had to offer me.

I gained strength to stand on my own, patted my own back and became my only support system. I was the only person who loved me and encouraged me.

I gave up on sacrificing time for you and only dedicated time to my work. The passion I once had for you began to be poured into my dreams.

It's crazy how my dreams have come true and you are no longer the woman of my dreams.

I've always believed that very few will support you until you make it. You made it clear to me that very few will be a fan before I have fans.

I don't know if you watched everything come together from afar. Seeing me become a full time writer and entrepreneur with regret in your eyes while having, 'I should've have been there for him', in your thoughts. But I do hope you see that I had the courage to do what I am passionate about, despite all of the doubts and odds.

It is unfortunate that you couldn't be my cheerleader and that we could not build a great team together. I guess my life happened and you were not in it.

I have no desire to rub anything in your face. I simply hope that choosing to be there for myself and be my own supporter inspires you to find your passion and chase your dreams as well, pushing aside every discouraging soul who wants to stop you.

We all need support, especially when we are trying to do something we love. In a world where they tell you to settle for less and to be mediocre, it is difficult when you decide to go against the norm and follow your dreams. There is almost a rebellion in the eyes of those who have accepted the fact that dreams don't become a reality, with no imagination to wish upon. Often times, those who do take the route of success, need a support system. When you have someone by your side cheering you on, it helps tremendously. To have someone encourage you to keep going during the times you are discouraged and receiving moral support from someone, can only help you as you follow your dreams.

Many have made it without the support of those they wanted to believe in them, even though I am sure that they wished differently. I can only imagine how hard it can be not to have anyone to truly celebrate with; no one to share precious moments and milestones with. It is human instinct to get excited about good news and to share it. That is why social media is full of posts about people's accomplishments. They want *someone* to know; it makes them feel better. For many, the support system they wish that they had includes family and friends. For those with partners, it's often their lover. It can be rough when the person who is supposed to be by your side, refuses to be there when you need them to be.

Do not listen to those who tell you your dreams are too big, unreachable and silly, they are those who gave up on theirs and will become those who criticize you when you do make it.

As a child, I was always doubted, I was the underdog. I was made fun of for being Haitian, in a foreign land where I did not speak English. I learned English by watching cartoons to grasp a bit more than what school was offering. I fixed that issue faster than most, then my accent became the new thing to laugh at by others. I was mocked for mispronouncing words and occasionally using a word out of context. I fought hard to perfect that and did for the most part, although my accent can be heard even now, it is nowhere near where it used to be. This may seem miniscule, but it was the beginning of fighting my own battles and feeling like I had to do many things alone.

When I became a runner, I can never say people doubted my talent in my earlier days. But when it came to races in the beginning, I was never known or expected to win, but I believe I was a threat because I was fast with great endurance. For the most part to others, I was just another person at the race not to worry about. I was an underdog, my team was the underdog and my town was full of underdogs.

I grew up in a small town named, Immokalee, located in southwest Florida. It is an agricultural town full of migrant workers and kids who lacked resources all across the board. Kids growing up there are often doubted, put into a stereotypical box that says, "You probably won't graduate, but if you do, you will end up in the fields like your parents picking watermelon or tomatoes."

I beat that stereotype. Being underestimated was nothing; odds stacked against me were not going to stop me. I was once told that many do not make it far from this town and that football was the main way out. I was not a football player; I was a runner. Instead of following the path which they said was the only one that would lead to success; I used my talent and my brain to land myself into college, earning one of the biggest scholarships of my class. It was not a running scholarship, but without being an elite runner, it wouldn't have been possible. I went to a college that wanted my talent, yet chose to evaluate me through the lens of academics.

By the time I became an adult, I was used to rising from nothing with almost no one cheering me on. It caused me to put people second to chasing success, somewhat pushing me to put materialism before love.

When I started to get in serious relationships, I was fresh out of college looking for work. I invested a lot of time on Twitter and created a fan base. As my fan base grew, I noticed I had a voice and had the desire to use the fan base to achieve more, impact others with words. My girlfriend at the time thought it had potential and started to support me.

Being at a different stage in life during those days, I was living with her and we started struggling financially. The fact that I was looking to build a brand online with a part time job wasn't cutting it for her. It was more of 'get up and find more to do with your life' instead of trying to be online-famous. She never cared to ask me what my focus was nor did she try to find out deep down what I wanted out of this, she simply wanted me to provide.

At that stage, I understood it was my responsibility as a man and had no problem looking for a job, but I rebelled because she did not seem to care enough or believe enough. I saw potential, I saw something that excited me, something that she felt I was wasting my time on. It hurt my feelings. The relationship ended and for quite a bit of time, her lack of support discouraged me. I began to lose my grip on what I wanted. I found myself a new job and while maintaining that job, I started to go after this passion of mine with a different focus. Mentally, I was aiming to prove her wrong, but my priority was sharing my gift to help others.

Following that relationship, I spent quite some time single, as always, to get myself together. The focus was me, my finances and building this brand called "Gentlemenhood". Surprisingly, a new relationship came into my life out of nowhere, and it had great potential. I was financially stable enough, had a better perspective on dating and was willing to make sacrifices. Soon enough, my partner could not accept the fact that I would share time that belonged to her with my passion.

Being a bit more mature than in my previous relationship, I did not get automatically defensive. It was my first instinct, but I controlled myself. It was hard to believe that another person would come into my life only to doubt something that I wanted for myself. I did not want to give up my dreams for a soul to love me. However, I understood her point of view. She wanted me to find balance, when I was head over heels in love with what I was doing and did not want much time to be away from it. I did my best to balance, but eventually lost grip of one of them.

I started to care for her deeply and did not want my relationship to head the same route as the previous one so I gave up on the idea, setting aside my aspirations. Things got better with her, but not for long. Soon after setting my brand aside, I launched into a new venture. I figured if I started something while with her, she would recognize that choosing her over my previous progress was a great sacrifice. I was hoping that she would compromise and support me on this new endeavor.

I was wrong, she couldn't see what I saw in this business venture, neither was she willing to support it. Soon enough, it started to come between us and our relationship went south and so did the business. We argued about it; we disagreed. She fought about my decisions and we threatened to leave each other. I grew to feel as if I was alone again, closing every door that could be open for her to participate if she wanted to. I started to fake being tired, trading my quality time with her, for business time. As a hard worker I was applauded for my drive, by strangers, while the woman who was supposed to be my favorite cheerleader was on the sideline booing me.

Our relationship started to die from there. Although many things led to us breaking up, her lack of support for my new enterprise was at the root of it. It was the cancer that killed what we had. It cut me deeply that I sacrificed my brand for her, only for her to not compromise and be by my side when I needed her. It was a hard pill to swallow, but we were no longer.

Eventually, I went back to rebuilding my brand, carrying out this ideology that many men live by, 'Success over love'. My brand did indeed flourish and it is the reason why you're currently reading this story.

As you read a summarized version of me chasing dreams while in a relationship, it is obvious that I did not suffer or endure as much discouragement as countless other men face. But, I can honestly say it was tough. The lack of support from the only person who I expected to be by my side when no one else was, was very discouraging. And, it sometimes led me to bitterness and a great amount of animosity towards women.

Lack of partner support from a woman is more of a common issue that men face than people would like to believe. I have seen it destroy enough relationships, weakening some of the strongest men. I've seen men build mountains of resentment because their woman only speaks doubts in their ears. It is hard to believe that someone really loves you and wants to spend their life with you, but what matters to you doesn't seem to matter to them. That goes against love.

There are already enough people and things keeping men from being who they want to be in this world, so to have the last person they can count on to believe in them, taking everyone's route of disbelief is brutal. Our partners ought to be our biggest fans, they may use wisdom to evaluate the path we choose, but they must also be supportive.

Too often, women want their men to support them, but do not want to reciprocate their support. Someone asked me once, "Why do some men sacrifice love and sometimes family for success?" I replied to them, "Either it is because the family or lover never supported them and they went on to do it alone with the mindset that 'I don't need anyone' or it's the only sense of confidence they have, the only thing that makes them feel significant." Greed and being a materialistic person can be right in there also, but to neglect lovers and family to the highest degree, often means that it's your form of revenge towards them. As men, it may seem as if we do not need support or crave the applause. But we do need the pat on the back and approval. There is nothing like these actions coming from someone who you love, your woman.

An island I've been good enough to discover, but never could find my way off it.

A place where hope is watered but never grows.

A cemetery, where many good guys lie lifeless from committing suicide and resurrecting the soulless versions of themselves.

I called this place home before. Somewhere I never thought I would ever be trapped in it until I caught myself banging on the cell bars, asking a few women at different occasions to set me free and hold their heart's captive.

This place is a prison cell for those who commit crimes of loving a good woman, while that woman allows thieves with bad intentions to steal all that she has to offer.

-   ***Let's be friends***

Friend-Zoned

I quietly played my position while this woman patiently played hers.

I was waiting for my turn, while she was waiting for the man she wanted to have her heart, to get it together.

We spent time together, shared moments with one another and had plenty of laughter together.

She wasn't convinced enough to stop fighting for another man who didn't want her because of the good moments. The enjoyment for him was in the pleasure of having her chained to his feet, dragging her behind him wherever he walked.

She was blind and starved for love, her hunger was only being nourished by the crumbs of acceptance that he left for her to eat from.

Every time they rekindled their relationship, it would lead to them breaking up and her refusing to give him a break.

During the times spent together, it was evident to her that I saw the good in her and she saw me for the good man that I had become.

She would say things like, "You're my best friend," and "Any woman would be lucky to have you," or, "All women need is a man who listens to them," etcetera.

The irony would be heavy on her breath as she said those things. I was the perfect idea of a boyfriend, but not the boyfriend she wanted or the man she needed though I fit the description of what she needed.

And when I politely asked her for her love, she replied "We've grown too close."

I tried to understand her view, but it seemed to be only backwards logic.

How can you find what you're looking for, yet close your eyes and say there must be better out there, and grab on to the worst?

The unfortunate thing is that it wasn't the first time, but one of the few times that I've been in a situation like this.

I was a perfect friend, would make a perfect boyfriend, but I could only be a friend to those women.

Although she was unwilling to admit it, she wanted the forbidden fruit. She wanted the man who excited her with a good amount of bad, the one who would bring some chaos into her life.

Her heart didn't have the doors open for a man like me, the friend zone was where I ended, though I had no intentions of being there.

I was led on by connection yet dropped by her decision. I could only be a friend to her, besides that's what I've been all along, but now without hope.

The friend-zone exists. It's quite often noticeable to everyone except for the person who's trapped in it. As a man who has played the role of the good guy more than the villain, I've considered it the 8th Wonder of the World. It never made sense to me why a woman would choose to put a good man to the side and entertain the bad man, yet complain about the quality of a relationship that the man she chose is offering her. It's almost the same as this crazy social media concept that we have today where someone chooses to follow someone, yet complains about what the person is posting. As if it's not the person's prerogative to post what they please. Yet, those who follow choose to keep up with their lifestyle that they do not agree with.

It seems as though they want love, yet they would rather try to suck it out of someone who doesn't naturally have it for them. I once believed this to be a sign of immaturity, when it's not really a direct reflection of someone's maturity level, but the stage where they are in terms of their understanding of love. I've seen a fair amount of women who are presently mature in many other aspects of life, yet they hang on to terrible fellas. Not because they are foolishly in love, but because there's a sense of false hope in there, being watered down by the men they choose to be with. It is so unfortunate, but it is just humans being humans, wanting what we can't have while rejecting or neglecting what we can have.

During the times that I became a prisoner trapped in the friend-zone, I only stayed because of intentions. Mentally I didn't feel stuck and unaccomplished as many would think. I believed in the power of consistency and persistency, so I invested time and effort only with the thought that it would reap me great results. Though there are men stuck in friend-zones under these conditions, I did not stay there as a man who was desperate, but as one keeping an eye open for opportunity. I thought that more was to come and the women made me believe that it was possible.

Once I realized nothing could come from what I was working for, the dilemma became knowing when to give up or when to keep fighting. Great love stories were often derived from friendship that caught on fire. I was trying to find out how much spark was needed for the fire to start. Believing that the better man would always win also kept me chained in these situations. I would come close often, but simply failed. It's a cycle I had to accept existed and that it was possible to fall victim to subconsciously.

Being stuck in different friend-zones before had an effect on me for a while, clouding my vision of what a woman really wants and how a man ought to be. It was a facilitator when it came to me forfeiting 'the good guy' role and living by the bad guy's lifestyle. The whole transformation and transition I spoke of in *Unspoken Feelings of a Gentleman*. To see women pass up a good man who will do anything for them and instead grab onto the bad one, had me believing that it's a bad man's world that good men can't win in. Not only did I play the role of a bad man for a few years to gain acceptance, I was convinced that women only want men who can break their hearts and those who want to cherish their hearts can only be friends with them.

There is a dilemma on both sides of this friend-zone idea. There are many good men incarcerated there, with substantial evidence that says they are victims of being led on. These men grow hopeful, only to become members of a friend-zone club. However, there are some who are there simply because they force themselves there, guilty of foolish choices.

There are instances when women are clear about having no interest in a man and the man proceeds to pursue her with the idea that persistence will always prevail. Unfortunately, that is not the truth. Persistency only prevails if there is interest. No interest means just that, no interest and those men need to understand that. Men who place themselves in the friend-zone due to their disobedience and unwanted choices are not victims. Being a patient wolf waiting on your prey to be available, isn't the same as being robbed of an opportunity you believe that you deserve.

Those who are in the friend-zone must learn to free themselves and understand that some women don't come to their senses until the men they friend zoned are gone and some women never come to their senses at all. To remain by her side hoping she turns around may work for some, but quite often it is painful and leads to depression with others. There are women out there who have come to their senses and will not let a good man go, even if they cut her hands off. A man must learn that he can be more than enough for some, but not enough for others. It's all based on what the other person is looking for. Staying in a situation that has no hope is the same thing as a woman holding onto or chasing men who are no good for her.

Don't become the dog that no matter what she does, he never gets on his feet and walks. Becoming a woman's pet is not the way to become the love of her life. Love waits, yes, but it does not wait forever. There's a time to complain about being in the friend-zone with a woman you want the best for, but there's also a time where the same complaining becomes whining. There is a fish out there for everyone, but you must go to the right river or pond at the right time.

Men aren't always villains who abuse love.

Sometimes they are victims hurt by what presented itself as love.

They are at times condemned by unhealed women and persecuted by those who seek revenge for the crimes their exes have committed.

It's easy for hurt women to live by the double standard that says men aren't good.

But it's not easy for men who are victims of that double standard, suffering for being different-for being actual men.

There are nights that it cuts me to know she's serving her heart to someone else who isn't me.

On those nights, I fall asleep, loving the fact that she is able to love again.

On those nights, I find joy at the thought that she's able to smile again, even though the person making her smile is a clown.

Those are the nights; I feel like a father letting his daughter do something the mother wouldn't approve of or wouldn't allow, but did it anyway because her daughter is young.

On those nights, I am happy knowing that she is happy.

Could she be making a mistake? Perhaps, but I've lived and learned that people love learning the hard way, from experiences they could've prevented if they sat and listened to wisdom.

It's unfortunate, that he will not love her the way I've loved her, but I've had my try.

- ***Someone Else***

If I could travel back in time, I would tell the young me to live young, but think old.

I've made plenty of mistakes without thinking and some from overthinking.

The biggest of them all was cheating on a woman who wouldn't cheat me out of an ounce of love; the second was expecting her to forgive me on my own timing.

Cheater's Remorse

My days became filled with frustration and my nights were filled with wet dreams, sleeping in the pool of my tears while dreaming of you.

On some days, I realized what I had done and that I deserved what I was suffering.

I think of how I would never let my own daughter return to a man who did not love her enough to stay faithful.

On other days, my selfishness would scream, wondering what is taking you so long to forgive me.

I said I am sorry, and I stopped blaming you for suffocating me with your love to a point where I felt I needed to run to other lovers to find freedom.

You act as if you don't want to talk to me, yet I know you spy on me.

You play CIA, monitoring my every move through social media and mutual friends.

You act as if you are over me, but in each other's presence your teary eyes spell I miss you.

You pretend as if you are okay, while deep down inside, you've yet to accept the fact that I can be cruel and trash your heart as if it's not worth treasuring.

You're wrong for leaving me, although I made this decision after much planning.

I didn't plan this part out; I didn't consider your feelings nor put much thought in the possibility of getting caught.

I was like a dumb thief who was clever enough to figure out how to break in, but not clever enough to create an escape plan or a plan B.

My eyes were fixated on the act. I was blinded by my desires and lust watered my hormones, clouding my mind with nothing but excitement, dreaming about the thrill.

The thought of your feet gaining strength to walk away never crossed my mind, not once.

My selfishness convinced me that I deserved this, as a man I figured variety is a necessity, I stayed faithful long enough so why not try it now.

At least give me credit for the time I held strong, when I said I love you, I meant it for the moment.

I grow angry when you don't answer my texts knowing you read them. We can still talk about this, communication can help, right?

I write these long texts saying I am sorry even though I don't like expressing myself.

I've gone to extreme measures to show you I'm sorry, I've embarrassed myself trying to show you that I love you.

Why are you doing this? Why are you playing hard to get?

Why won't you take me back?

Why is it taking you so long to get over this?

Quite often when a man cheats, we want remorse. We expect forgiveness immediately. As the world continues to be a place where people live by self-entitlement, our egos can convince us that we do not have to be accountable for our foolish choices. Many of us don't want the blame nor are we willing to accept the fruit of the consequences. Even a man who is a responsible adult sometimes finds it hard to be responsible for his cheating act.

As men, we are quick to point out the areas where a woman failed to meet her end of the bargain and say that her actions are what influenced our decisions. It has become common that when a woman finds evidence that a man is cheating, the man points out the fact that it's wrong of her to be searching, switching the focus to her decision.

Demanding remorse and immediate forgiveness without a shadow of a doubt lives in both genders, but as men we've milked it more. Blame is something that is rooted in humans since the beginning; it exists due to the sinful state of mankind. Even Adam blamed Eve for his wrong doing and Eve blamed the serpent. If you follow the allegorical story carefully, you will see that Adam attempted to guilt God by saying, "The woman you gave me." Adam was hinting that not only was it the woman's fault, but God also had a part in it, rejecting accountability from two angles.

Unfortunately, even in modern times we have found a way to nurture the blame even more. Women have been conditioned to attack the other woman their man is cheating with, instead of the man whom they have a relationship with. They get hurt by their man, yet blame the woman involved. Some go as far as fighting the other woman over something that their man allowed. It is the man who owes his woman faithfulness, not the woman he cheated with. Although the other woman should respect another' person's relationship, they aren't obligated to. The accountability falls on the person who you're in a relationship with, the one who betrayed you. There are many cases where the other woman truly does not know that they were the side piece.

> **Many cheaters are not sorry for hurting their partner. They are sorry for getting caught, which sabotages their plan of keeping their relationship as an unfaithful person.**

A man cheating is a man's fault, besides; a man doesn't become a cheater in a split second. They may not have thought it through all the way, but it was in the works. To cheat takes time to numb the guilt and make it okay unless they are habitual cheaters. The times I have cheated, I started with justifying what I looked at and the little things I did. I convinced my heart that it was okay, so when the opportunity arose I acted. It became easy for me to shift blame towards my woman when caught, condemning her for not quickly putting aside what happened and forgiving me. Because by the time it was done, I had counseled myself to a point where I believed what I was doing was okay, but reminded myself that I could not get caught.

I have been the idiot who ruined a good relationship and became genuinely sorry. Once everything goes downhill, all one can think about is apologizing and waiting for her to forgive and bring the relationship back, without thinking about what was actually done or about the consequences . It can be hard dwelling on the thought that you made the wrong decision and what that decision will cost you, or that your relationship could be no more. Doing whatever is necessary to restore things becomes the primary objective and when seeing no progress or results, one tends to freak out. It is why a man will send a woman countless beautiful messages in the morning, thousands of apologies, and occasionally do little things to convince her that he loves her. Then all of a sudden, he flips and goes to the opposite end of the spectrum, getting angry at the woman, pointing out her flaws and expressing how good she isn't.

You can't stab someone in the heart and get mad at them for bleeding and then grow angry when their heart isn't healing as fast as you want it to. Infidelity is hard on people. We must put ourselves in the shoes of those we hurt to see how they feel. It's hard for any man to even picture their woman cheating on them with another man, better yet forgiving her for such a thing. But we demand that. It's easy for us to ask others to give grace for our sins, yet we condemn them for theirs and believe that they should be punished for their crime.

To the man in this situation: If you love this woman as you claim, leave her alone. Give her time to heal. The more you keep trying to show her you are sorry and willing to change, the more you will push her away. You can't hurt people and expect them not to mourn or put an expiration date on their mourning. You may think consistently reaching out to her is showing her you will fight to win her back and will not give up easily, but my friend, it is annoying her.

What she needs is her space. She may not mean it when she says, "Leave me alone," but she deserves a break from you. Suffocating her will lead her to truly wanting to be left alone. She deserves at least some moments to think alone and have a little peace without you interrupting it. You are the reason she is currently suffering, you aren't the remedy at the moment, you are simply a thorn in the wound. Yes, a woman or anyone will say things that they don't mean when they are hurt, but that's not the time to use persistence to manipulate her or force your way back in. It's unfair to her and evil of you. Use that time to make necessary changes if you want her.

Change the habits that have influenced your poor decisions that put her through this to begin with. Make adjustments and modify your behaviors. If you truly loved that woman, you know she deserves the best of you, so don't try to make her believe in the same you who trashed her heart. Focus on working on you and give her time. You may think it's wise to show her any progress you've made, but it will most likely remind her of the fact that you didn't do those things in the relationship. Leave that woman alone as you leave that old you behind. As time passes by she will see the change if she wants to and she will find reasons to give you a second chance.

To the woman caught up in such a situation: A man does not cheat because you drive him to cheat. A man cheats because he isn't disciplined enough to fight lust, he's insecure or simply just a cheater who doesn't love you.

As a married man who has healed from quite a bit, I can tell you that the desire to cheat isn't there when you love someone. Lust however will tempt a man, but the man should do whatever is necessary to win against that lust if he is truly in love. No one purposely does things that will destroy who or what they love. Whatever it is, it is internal. You cannot blame yourself for their decisions nor should you crucify yourself for wanting to free yourself from them. Having them beg for second chances doesn't mean they deserve a second chance. The man who does indeed deserve a second chance (which are few), will prove to you that they do. They will make life-altering changes that should be seen.

If a cheater is trying to force you to believe that they have changed, it is because they really have not. Forcing it upon you is a clear indicator that he doesn't believe in that change. He is using a convincing method which a changed man doesn't need to use. A man who has truly changed will wait/hope that you detect those changes when the opportunity presents itself.

You may not have been a perfect partner, but that does not mean that it's your fault. If someone is unhappy being with you, they should leave the relationship, they should not cheat. Put your focus on moving forward and healing. Seeking revenge will only cause more damage to what's left, if there's anything left and it will hurt you more. The best revenge is to love yourself enough to move forward without trying to prove anything. Don't try to restore things when you are hurt. Letting him back in during the time you are still mourning his choice, will be torment to you both. Go your separate ways and if it's meant to be, the path will lead back to each other, but do not force it.

Also, you may still care for someone despite all of the wrong that they have done to you. No one simply stops caring, people may pretend, but it's almost impossible if they truly cared to begin with. Therefore, it's perfectly fine if you care, but do not let those emotions allow you to jump back into his arms when you have every reason not to. Fight those emotions and cry it out until all of the pain leaves you in liquid form. Let the anger out or vent on paper if you have to. The sooner you forgive him the better, but the sooner you forgive yourself, the sooner freedom will find you.

*I've heard the same people who say:
"Don't judge me by my past," say: "Once
a cheater, always a cheater."*

*I've seen those who scream, "Your
mistakes do not define you," nod in
agreement with them.*

*I don't know if it's the smell of hypocrisy on
their breath or the ugly sound of the hurt
that is deep in their hearts when they talk
causing me to shake my head violently
when in their presence. But I've decided to
write them a note that reads, "People
change, you've done it and believe in it.*

*What you need to change is whatever
makes you believe that you're the only
one who is capable of changing."*

-      **People Change**

Prison Sentence

I came into your life and caused chaos,

I picked the lock to the door of your heart and sabotaged everything inside like a thief with much anger inside of him.

You trusted me and I walked all over that trust as if it were the welcome rug in front of many homes.

I lied, I cheated, I manipulated you, only to have regret drag me back on my knees begging you for forgiveness.

Like most, I cried, I fought the pain and I even grew angry and recognized my faults.

Unlike many, I changed, bettered my habits and improved behaviors before I chased you again and pursued your heart.

Like many, I made promises, unlike many I kept them.

And it worked, you took me back.

You didn't only rely on your emotions and feelings, but you used your brain this time.

You saw a different version of me come to life, you saw love in my eyes and showed compassion towards me.

I felt lucky and blessed to receive a second chance to have my woman back, after hurting her.

A dream come true it was, but then I started seeing the nightmares.

You forgave me with your heart, but your memory kept account of my bad choices.

You let go of the past, but held on to what it taught you.

You put me in a prison in our relationship, watching my every move, silently doubting every decision, and looking for anything that would confirm that I would return to my old ways.

I grew frustrated, tired, bothered,

I felt like an innocent prisoner who was being wrongfully convicted for crimes he didn't commit, simply because of his past.

Why?

Why did you take me back if you were going to put little effort into forgiving me?

Why did you let me back in if you'd quietly condemn me and place on the walls of your heart the old image of who I am?

Why did I suffer for doing good, simply because before I had done bad?

I knew that consequences and repercussions come with bad decisions, but never did I imagine it to be this, I thought it would be just me losing you.

Maybe I never got you back. Maybe you just wanted me in your palm to show me what it felt like to crush a heart that beats for you.

Whatever it was, I became tired of this prison. I was tired of serving this sentence.

In the end, all I wanted was for you to free me, or at least try to forgive me, if your plan was to just keep me there.

The thing about second chances is that we all deserve them, but in many cases, not with the same person. It's a common thing that people take relationships lightly, growing too comfortable and taking their partner for granted. In many cases, men allow their immaturity and lustful desires to take them down a route that only sabotages their relationship. They often jeopardize something good for temporary moments of thrills or something less.

> ## People deserve forgiveness but not all those you forgive deserve a second chance.

A good number of those destroyed relationships are reparable, but more of them are not. Repairing a relationship is more than getting back into the relationship; it's the effort that is put into it once you get back into it. It often requires more work than you have put in before, since you are completely rebuilding rather than building. As men, we fail to realize that sometimes the residue of pain stays in a woman's heart once we hurt her, even when she says she forgives us. It is nearly impossible for many people to forgive without hanging on to the memories and the damage it caused. It takes a miracle or some quality time with God and spiritual growth. It's hard for many women to completely forgive their partner and even harder for them to forgive themselves.

Forgiving the man is usually the first stage. It is often a difficult task, but not the hardest. What lingers around in a woman's mind and haunts her, is usually the memory of allowing herself to fall into such a situation. That can keep just about anyone stuck in the past while trying to put themselves in drive to go forward.

The overwhelming power of doubt becomes extremely strong, consistently beating happiness in a match of arm wrestling. Doubting that the person can offer honesty becomes the only handcuff, while doubting whether they are worthy of love or were loved before becomes the shackles around their feet. Trusting again is a hard thing once you have been hurt. Unnecessary walls that feel necessary are built to prevent what happened from happening again. Being with the person who hurt them before becomes a painting of what torment looks like and it is all they can see when they look at the person. Sometimes the best and most loving choice is letting each other go free and onto a separate journey.

> **Relationships can only be restored if there's full forgiveness; full forgiveness is forgiving and forgetting. Unless you put the experience in the past and use the lesson wisely, forgiving becomes only a word instead of an act.**

As hurt women struggle to forgive themselves, some of them pull the man back into the relationship. They grant him another chance, while they are still not healed. It becomes torture for the man because hurt people, hurt people. Sometimes without the thought of revenge in mind, the relationship becomes all about it. Everything he does becomes suspicious and he is monitored to prevent things from happening as they did before. As a man who took necessary steps to make some changes and improve his behavior, I can tell you that it is frustrating when someone no longer sees your potential. The claim is that a woman is being given the benefit of the doubt, when all the while he is being doubted. It's almost as hurtful as being cheated on and can sometimes feel worse.

If a man isn't prepared to endure a great amount of hardship and experience the part of love that requires endurance, a second chance isn't what he needs even if he believes that he deserves it and says he will work for it. It's hard for any human being to constantly feel like a failure without giving up, but it is much harder when it's his own fault. Restoration is hard work; people have to be willing to go against a tsunami of doubt flowing out of a heart that is broken to make it happen. Couples who come out on the other side usually become stronger because it takes quite a bit of time and a lot of patience.

However, we must learn that some things aren't fixable even if we fix ourselves. The consequences for our mistakes are sometimes the end of something great. Becoming better to be better to someone who was hurt is common, but that better version may not be what the other person needs or wants. The hardest lesson life gives sometimes is to force a person to lie in the bed that they made, but after waking up, things can become better. Being a better person isn't defined by becoming what the woman needs the man to be, it's defined by his growth. Being better doesn't always restore our loss. Sometimes we get restored and hold onto the consequences, but also learn a lesson to carry us to better places.

I am not jealous, I am afraid and fear sometimes makes me territorial.

I don't want to see what I invested my heart into get stolen.

I am well aware no one can steal a woman who is truly mine, but the fact is; I am still willing to protect what is mine and will act when I feel it is threatened.

It is hard for me to act like I don't care if she leaves only as reverse psychology.

I've seen it work magic, a man pretends the woman isn't worth much to him and that woman fights to convince him she is worthy.

Although often times it is reverse psychology, but sometimes it is not reversed at all.

Sometimes, It is a person reacting to the fact that they have watched some people leave before.

I tried to convince myself to never care that much and never try to stop another person from leaving. It takes too much energy to keep them if they don't want to stay.

*I used to push people away to never grow
to care, but now I care more, which is
where the jealousy comes from.*

- **Jealousy**

Move On

I am strong enough to let things go, unlike many men I've known.

Those men have let the memories become nightmares that keep them from reaching their dreams, while the thought of finding the woman of their dreams is brutally beaten by the knuckles of their failed experiences.

Letting go is not a boomerang, they will not automatically come back.

Letting go is more like letting a bird fly away on a summer's day without the thought that it would return. It may find its way back or find freedom in being free, but it never comes back to the place you believe ought to be its home.

Letting go makes one realize that what once brought happiness will no longer do so, but it will become what keeps someone else smiling. That must be searched for twice as much, with twice as much caution for someone who can bring that happiness back to your life.

Even the strongest men are sometimes too weak to let go.

It takes a courage that forces one to accept the cold reality. It grabs them in the fashion of a police officer making an arrest of an uncooperative suspect, mandating that they change and make the past a memory.

Many try to hold on while pretending, locking their happiness away, while throwing the key at their exes begging them to open it.

It's unfortunate that many of us work much harder on pretending that we have let go than we actually put energy into doing so.

Many grow depressed trying to make sense of it by focusing on bank accounts, losing themselves in a bottle where waves of alcohol violently drown them, or trying to find closure in opened legs.

Women are known to hold on when the relationship is dead, while men, refuse to let go of the casket as the relationship is being buried.

We cry our eyes out in the last hour, as the lifeline is pulled forever.

We become what the relationship needed once the woman no longer has need of us.

It's painful to accept that what was will never be once again, but it has to be treated as bad tasting medicine, nasty but healthy and necessary.

Moving forward requires being free from the past and takes more courage at times, because it is an act of love towards oneself and that woman.

Finding such freedom is what many men need, but will look for in the wrong places for a while and some will never find it.

Many men are strong physically, but out of those men, more than enough of them aren't strong emotionally. How can it be so, when men on most occasions are the first to get over the relationship? Men have faster legs than women, they sprint out of relationships, however their emotions are a bit slower to leave. The emotional side of things is usually something that hits us (men) last, simply because we've learned and been conditioned to put emotions last.

When my sisters and I found out that my mother had cancer, they all broke down and cried right there. I stood there calm and collected. It hit me like a ton of bricks, but did not really register until my mother went to her appointment that would lead her to having surgery. I cried harder than my sisters when I was alone, when I truly realized what was going on and processed it properly; digesting it emotionally. This happened when I buried my father as well. It wasn't until I had to let go of the casket as it was going down that it registered emotionally that I would never see him anymore. I screamed and cried, violently holding the casket with a tight grip.

This is akin to how many men deal with relationships ending. Quite often after the break up, they are fine and doing everything they wanted. Enjoying the single life, until months or even years later, they process the break up emotionally, starting to mourn the loss and then they start trying to restore things. That time is usually too late, when everything has reached its final points, when the ex decides to start seeing someone or anything else that happens as a clear indication that there is no longer a chance.

There are countless men who never truly process their heartbreaks emotionally, they never move on, but live as if they have. Many men cannot have healthy relationships simply because they are carrying the pain from their first relationship that went sour. Some refuse to love any woman back because their ex still has their heart subconsciously. No different than women, men hold grudges, men grow bitter, and often times bottle up emotions and throw the hurt down at the bottom of a bottle. Instead of guarding their hearts to never repeat the experience that burned a whole through it, they guard the pain and use it as fuel to make women suffer. Numerous women fall victim to these men because the men refuse to receive love from them.

There was a point in my life where love wasn't welcomed, sex was the only form of love I knew and wanted. It was the easiest way to protect myself from getting my heart broken. It was well over three years since my ex discontinued our relationship, but almost every day, I wanted to show her that it could work. I ventured into the mourning stages too late, breaking my own heart over the fact that I couldn't do anything to restore it. It took me years before the thoughts about her, the anger, and burning desire to find someone whom I believed she would consider a quality pick, would stop. I used this desire to prove to her that I could do better. I rejected women of great potential to get with a couple whom would be great tools for jealousy. I was living in misery, until I said, "Enough is enough."

Some grown men still try to get with their middle school girlfriend, while others try to rekindle an old high school relationship or attempt to get another chance with a girlfriend from years ago. As a life coach who has had female clients, I often hear stories of long time exes popping up in the picture. It can be unusual and confusing to women, yet I see it as men being men. We, as men, tend to hold on to history and keep what has not been for too long, trying to make it what *is*.

Men's competitive nature in many cases doesn't help. Men can have a real problem with losing, which doesn't allow them to accept the fact that they have lost. Instead, they fight without purpose or hope, but hunger to be in the position they once were.

Loneliness

They think it's only women who grow desperate for love

As if longing for love so bad can't make your heart itch, your emotions becoming a misbehaving child. Crying for things not needed and every bone in you wanting someone, whether it's settling or not, is not only a woman's pain.

The idea that men are fine with being single; that loneliness does not know their address when boredom has them captive or during sleepless nights or unoccupied weekends, is as true as saying death is avoidable.

Loneliness tried to bully me countless times, showing me pictures of friends with partners, couples out and about and sweet memories of my old relationships.

Social media and video games kept my attention at times to keep me from turning my neck as loneliness called, but they never provided enough companionship to override the desire to be in the presence of a woman.

I've seen some numb it with alcohol and others use a promiscuous lifestyle or the more innocent approach of having a pool of 'text buddies'.

Those are only Band-Aids though; they only work for so long.

As men, we love affection, but won't admit that we crave it.

We love being cared for, but many of us won't complain of it.

We want love, but we won't show that we have a need for it.

Loneliness picks on some of us quite often and it tags desperation to intensify the torment.

We are not immune to it; some of us simply live our lives in denial, treating it as a myth and some of us find ways to heal and befriend patience.

Loneliness is a painful journey, one that takes many on a rampage of desperation, committing crimes against people's hearts. It is also a good friend of depression, helping that demon suck the life out of people. Loneliness is a real deal, especially in the modern world where people are always seeking something and spending great amounts of time staring at others' relationships finding new, 'relationship goals'. It's too often believed that men are not a species that gets lonely, as if it's a myth about them, versus an absolute reality for women. Perhaps it is because men show less emotion, rarely voicing their needs. However, loneliness visits a great amount of men as well.

As humans we all crave companionship, as society wrongfully teaches us that we should never voice our emotional needs. We scream, "I need companionship", but with a different tone in a different language than women do.

Many men become players because they cannot cope with the loneliness. It is better for them to chase countless women, keeping constant interaction with them and feeding off of their attention, rather than staying still being patient until love shows up at their door steps. It's obvious that many women jump from relationship to relationship as a method to deal with their loneliness as well. Yet, as men, many of us prefer keeping ourselves occupied, rather than continuously investing in ourselves and becoming attached. Therefore, we build a list of texting buddies, or friends with benefits convincing as many women as we can lure, to believe that we want a committed relationship, while only playing a game.

Though it is not something only men do, they do it, as a way to cope with loneliness. The thrill of having new women and the pleasure of sex is primary when it comes to men playing women, but secondary is loneliness. When men choose the 'dog path', though it's an immature and corrupt part of him in action, it's mainly influenced by his need to be with someone. Men do far too much for women to impress them, to not feel as if something is missing without one. Even God felt something was missing when man was alone.

> **Almost all have faced the feeling of loneliness, but almost everyone chooses not to acknowledge or admit it.**

When I decided to let go of my old boyish ways, which included playing women and being inconsiderate to their hearts, I also started to walk as a born again Christian right after. Dating gained a new meaning to me, the goal of relationships was renewed to me and the purpose of approaching women was completely different. I no longer kept a list of women to meet my needs during the times I stayed single, nor did I have the urge to chase countless women with the wrong motive. I became a man waiting in my singleness, staying put and applying patience; respecting women enough to not approach them for any reason but to court them and to build a solid relationship that could head towards marriage.

While having this focus, my weekdays became short and my weekends became long and torturous. The times I wouldn't be at work were occupied with things such as working out, sleeping and watching television, leaving me very little time to process my singleness. During weekends however, I had nothing but time and being alone became more real. It became clear to me that I was without someone to be at the movies with, someone to hang out with, carry conversations with and journey into new adventures with.

At times I felt compelled to entertain a few women online, but could not go forward with the idea simply because of my convictions. Weekends seemed longer and at times I would slip into short periods of depression. I felt unwanted, though that wasn't the case. I felt unloved, as if no one cared for me since my desire for companionship wasn't being fulfilled. Besides, I was no longer on a constant chase to fulfill my selfish ways nor was I living the party life. That was once the remedy that numbed the pain of my reality.

Doubts filled my head, questioning why I was choosing to take a route even most women refused to take or so I believed. Being lonely was lame; the single life was a curse, without engaging in the search for companionship on a regular basis. Spending time with my friends was great at times, but they could not bring me the satisfaction of being with someone of the opposite sex who was full of interest and ready to water what is between us.

The thought of my previous relationships and moments with exes would walk their way back into my memory, whispering in my ear that there was fun in dating, and in trying out different people. All the while, begging me to abort my mission to be alone, growing and patiently waiting on who God had for me

Loneliness was real to me during those days. Before, it was something I'd seen women wrestle with, providing me with the opportunity to capitalize off of their vulnerability. I could not understand how much of a burden it could be on the mind until I decided to stop myself from actively dating while broken, like many others. Feeding myself ego food, yet destructive to the soul.

Being lonely is something normal that anyone can experience when they are without a partner. Unfortunately, some deal with these feelings even while they are in a relationship. Feeling lonely is not an issue that can be dodged throughout your lifetime. It's an emotion no different than feeling sad or happy. It is an emotion that is tough to overcome, when it's so easy to stare at those who have companionship through social media. Envy and jealousy can creep in. Bad intentions to pursue a partner or a relationship will find its way in to keep up with everyone.

The most precious thing a man can have by his side is a lady, but it can be hell seeing no one on your side or no one on your arm, as guys without morals do every other night. The feeling is real, but it must not dictate our choices. Men, as well as women, who find it hard to fight this battle with loneliness end up losing themselves in new relationships. The cure to loneliness is learning to be happy alone, to be patient and focus on you for the time being. Enough of us aren't true to ourselves enough to admit that there's something missing when we do not have someone, but we must learn to be true to ourselves and to wait for what we deserve when we deserve it.

There is both joy and regret when I see my ex while being with my current woman. The joy first started with me knowing that it hurt her to see that I've moved on and the regret is in knowing that she will no longer be mine and that the history is gone.

Now, the joy is in knowing we will be no longer and the history is gone because I found someone else. The regret now is in knowing that she is hurting when she sees me with my current, not because I care for her as a lover, but I still care for her as a person.

-    **Joy & Regret**

Forbidden Fruit

I want her back in my life,

I sometimes feel it is because she has lived here before in my heart and we had a thing close to what love is.

I am unsure why, but it feels as if it is the thing to do.

I do not get along with her parents and she craves their approval.

She used to say she loves me, but uncertainty sat heavy on those words.

And I've realized that I am no longer attracted to her, but to the memory of how beautiful she was, which keeps my imagination entertained and holding on, with the belief that better does not exist elsewhere.

At times, I cannot remember what I loved about her presence. We argued from the beginning, going back and forth wrestling with reasons why we could make it, reasons we ourselves didn't quite believe in, but we said them.

It was cursed from the start.

We spent most of our time on our cell phones, admiring other people's lives; while we watched ours go by and questioned our life together.

The rest of the time we spent together, we spent wishing for better days, rarely seeing the face of happiness.

Our conversations were empty and we exchanged words at times, just because silence scared us.

Sometimes I reminisce about the good times we did experience together, the trips, the dates. But when my emotions sober up, I remember how those things ended terribly. Arguing our way out of the most beautiful moments.

Our intimacy was sexual favors which we both knew as wrong, being people who believed in living pure before marriage, but we convinced ourselves that our desire for sin was greater than our willingness to do right. It was the only thing we could agree on and that made our time together pleasurable, if we were honest with ourselves.

The more I looked back, the more I saw that we had nothing in common but history.

We believed that every great couple faced opposition and that we could rise together; the thing is, we weren't great and the opposition was there before we began.

Our favorite song was, "I Won't Give Up", which was the perfect remedy to our situation. But we still played that song over and over, convincing ourselves to fight a battle that could never be won.

The more I reflect on us and what we used to be, the more I see what we couldn't see: the pain, the hurt, no compatibility and a story that could never be written as a love story. Yet, I am still here wanting you and wanting your heart.

It's as if your love was poison, but to me it was honey and we were bad for each other, but I couldn't stop craving you.

It's evident you're no longer the apple of my eye, but I am like Adam and you represent the apple that hangs from the tree.

People fight for things they don't need all the time. They hang on to things and people they are better without. They like to stick to what they had, because they had it, not because they need it. To say that men are the only ones who sometimes want what they can't have is foolish; but to say that men fight for a woman they can't have and don't need simply because they want to be in control is common sense.

We (men) do not like losing, it bruises our ego. We do not like to feel as if we lost a relationship and it haunts us. When we see challenge and opposition sometimes, our competitive nature dares us to take on the responsibility to show them that we can do it. Therefore, we sometimes do things just because we want to and feel if we do so, we will be accomplished.

I've been at a place where my relationship ended and I fought for it, knowing nothing productive could ever come from it. I registered that mentally, but emotionally I couldn't process it. I didn't want to process it. No one wants to tell themselves that they are wrong and what they are doing is without any good purpose, when they have a strong urge to do it. In every man's heart, whatever they are doing serves a purpose, whether it is right or wrong. To them it is most likely not wrong or purposeless.

Whether it was the woman's fault or my fault it didn't matter, I never wanted my relationship to end without a fight. I chased women before as a natural reaction to losing, it's what one does as a male sometimes, fighting to stay at the throne of a woman's heart whether it is deserved or not. You fight to do what they said you can't make happen, which is to change and to be better towards them.

There are quite a bit of men, right now at this very moment chasing a woman, simply because the pursuit is challenging. These types of men see rejection as the first bump to a great quest. There are quite a bit more at this very moment chasing a woman they once had, attempting to get her back without even asking themselves why. They don't find it a necessary thing to do. Whether they love her or not sometimes doesn't even matter.

Chasing the forbidden fruit is something many men do to apply the power of persistency and provide nourishment to their ego. It's not uncommon to hear men say, "*I can get more girls than you,*" with other males applauding each other for being able '*to pull that*', which means they crossed over any barrier a woman had to keep men like them away.   Persistency helps many men get the woman who said "no" to them. It may be because that man truly wants the woman and pictures a life with her. But, there are countless times that it's simply because that man wants a great catch. It's not a big deal to numerous fellas to go to desperate measures to get that woman who made it seem impossible to win her heart. We love and fight hard for what we want even though we're not willing to keep it, as long we want it, having it usually becomes a must.

When we lose our woman, the power of persistency and willingness to chase is another area where this logic comes to life. It's one thing to go after a woman who you believe to be playing hard to get, it's another thing when you had that woman and believe you can get her again. As men, we use the fact we've been with a person to convince ourselves that we must win them back and they owe us to come back to us because we had something.

A man wants his woman back for different reasons besides the fact she's no longer his and he feels the need to change that, that exists. Often time, it's for the sake of history. Holding on to what was, because they don't want to see all of it thrown away or taken by another man. There are plenty of instances where it's a form of revenge some men use, to make sure their ex suffers from the pain of heartbreak as well. I've seen those men lace up their shoes and chase the woman until he gains power over her emotions, then turns the table on her. There will always be various reasons why men chase after a woman he has had, sometimes it's even an emotional attachment. However, on more than enough occasions it is simply because the man can no longer have this woman freely, on his own terms.

I remember going after an ex whom I thought I was deeply in love with, failed attempt after failed attempt, I could only fight harder. Giving up on the relationship came across to me as the wrong decision. I couldn't find it in my heart to let go of what we had, everyone knew about it and may have loved it; it all seemed too right to let it go.

As someone who sits and evaluates, I finally looked in the mirror and asked myself, "Why do I even want to be with this woman?" As the question ran laps around my brain, I could not find valid reasons as to why. I only began to notice that I had already met better women for me. I deserved more than the relationship without depth she was willing to give me and a physical connection that kept me excited.

I then realized as well that, I kept trying harder only when she said we would never be with each other. I gained more strength to not give up when her mother said that we didn't belong together. I fought more and more for her when people said they doubted that we would work.

As I truly evaluated what I was doing, I realized I was never after her because of my love for her; it was about proving to people that they were wrong and that I could do this. It was about having what everyone says I should not have. When she started to make her way back to me, I would lose interest, but as soon as she drifted away again and I felt that I lost my grip on her, I would go back to fighting hard. The logic was no different than me always wanting to play outside when my mom didn't let me, as soon as I gained permission to do so, and then it was no longer something I desired. No resistance meant that I had no real interest. I didn't want this woman; I wanted what I believed should be. I wanted what I believed I could not have and should make happen. We, as humans, love to chase the forbidden fruit, simply because it's forbidden, not because the fruit is good for us.

I've experienced and observed many experiences where people do not see that this is what they are doing which can open a can of hurt, if one wasn't opened already. When men run after women because of the fact that she's what he can no longer have, many women eventually fall for their spell and become vulnerable once again. Giving in to the same men again, and becoming subject to painful heartbreaks leaves many women damaged and searching for closure. It's painful to have someone mislead you, it is torment to have them take your heart and say: "I won it," like it was a trophy, not because it was of value.

We do not think about our actions, nor do we think about the fruit of those decisions and some of us simply don't care. As men, we must learn to chase not for the purpose of winning or having, but to gain something we believe to be treasured, a good woman's heart. We must learn to let go of what didn't work and accept the loss. It will be beneficial both for us and for the women who have walked with us on our path.

I've held on to poisonous relationships before. Although I wanted nothing to do with those bad lovers, I could not convince my heart to remove the chains they had around the legs of my emotions.

Some call it holding on to memories, and others call it not giving up easily. But to me it was attachment, holding on to everything I felt for them and with them, refusing to set myself free.

- ***Emotional Attachment***

My Deceased Child

I cannot wait to meet you in heaven,

I hope I am not too busy apologizing when I am there.

Have you met my best friend, Gary?

Did you by any chance run into a man who looks just like me?

I do not know if my father crossed those gates, so I am asking.

How is it up there?

When we meet, I can't wait to hear what it's like to be in heaven all of your life.

When you were conceived, I was a coward who was full of himself.

At that time, I believed I was too young to handle the responsibility of having a child, but never did it cross my mind that I didn't consider myself too young to have sex.

I was a fool, who chose my lifestyle before your life.

I chose a more promising future rather than giving you a future.

How could I commit murder so freely, how could I be this selfish?

I wonder at times.

"At least I won't be like one of those dads who did not nurture his seed," I would say to myself, to numb the guilt.

My heart aches at times when I think that you could be living and breathing on this earth.

I will not be able to see you open your eyes for the first time, take your first step, say your first word.

I will never get the chance to know if you would say, "Mommy or Daddy", first or if you would grow to become an athlete, musician or a nerd in school.

Never will I find out what fruit my seed would bear, how many grandkids would come from you.

I will miss out on many events, just as you will.

Oh, how I wonder what my days would be like with you being in my life.

I denied you these things, I denied myself of so many moments.

The damage of aborting you may have been caused to your mother, but I will never know.

We do not talk anymore; she is a stranger that I once knew.

It's almost as if we never met, like me and you.

I am sorry my child; I did not know better.

I knew what I was doing, but did not know the meaning of it.

I assure you that my sins did not go without being repented.

On occasion you come to mind and I feel as if my hands are filled with blood, but I do not let those days take life out of me.

I thank God for the blood of Jesus and thank Him for forgiving me.

Until death comes to take life out of me or when Christ comes back, I will see you then my child.

I may not have loved you enough before, but know that I do love you.

Sincerely,

Your Changed Father

I once made a terrible mistake. That mistake was choosing abortion to bury the result of my decisions. I was on a hiatus from school and living back home filled with boredom. During those times, I believed sex to be the only fun available to young men like me. I still idolized those who got to drink, smoked and had sex. It was what many who were my age entering their early 20s, believed to be living the life.

As a young adult without a car, partying was out of the picture for me and the way my mother raised me, I knew better than to follow the smoking and drinking pattern. All that was available to me was sex. My mother did not approve of the promiscuous life, but she did not expect me to be a virgin. Therefore, I delved into that. I searched for women online (Myspace) and built meaningless relationships with them. Friends with benefits flooded my phone, a routine I was used to prior to that summer. As I enjoyed the benefits, I did not pay attention to what those benefits could bring into my life besides moments of pleasure.

It's obvious we live in a sowing and reaping universe. Somehow we don't think about it as if it is something obvious. I knew pregnancy was the fruit of unprotected sex, but never thought of the possibilities, never thought it would happen. I was more afraid of catching an STD at the time.

It happened during the summer before I headed back to college. I received a phone call from one of the women stating that she was pregnant. Somehow it shocked me. "This can't be happening," I said to myself. My first initial thoughts were: 'What would my mother think'? 'What would people think?' 'How would I take care of this baby?' The thought of the baby having a life wasn't even worth thinking about at the time. The woman and I both agreed an abortion would be the choice to make, so we made it happen. It was a relief, yet it hurt. I spent time wondering once everything was final and she and I were a closed chapter.

There are many males who choose to have abortions for a similar reason, their intention is to enjoy the fun in sex without thinking of the consequences and then it happens. Sex to them is nothing but pleasure, they aren't prepared for what could happen if having sex leads to what sex is primarily meant for. Instead of accepting the responsibility when it happens, they choose the shortcut. They choose to not let their daughter or son experience the opportunity of living.

As a man who myself is a miracle baby, I grew to sometimes question what would have happened if I had that child and chose the path of early fatherhood. As a spiritual person who understands that life was formed soon after the sperm fertilizes the egg, I sometimes question what that child looks like in heaven. I had few moments where I condemned myself and felt guilty for my choices, it was tough. I made that decision as an immature young man who did not put much thought into what I was doing, it was the best escape route. Although I did not know better or think much about it, the thought still came to haunt me at times. I can only imagine how it affected men like me who made such choices at a more mature stage in life.

No different than women, men feel similar pains because of abortion. The pain of the physical process we may never experience, but emotionally and mentally it haunts us. I do not know how many men feel this pain, but I know many of them are torn by miscarriage. Aborting a child is easy since you have never known them or are attached to them, but the act does leave some residue. Your imagination will create scenarios that will keep you wondering what could be. It may not be a long and lasting hurt, but one that visits sometimes during the days a man reflects.

Aggressor

I was not always the aggressor,

It may sound like a myth written on the pages of a book for those born yesterday, but I kid you not.

I was not always the initiator.

There were times I wanted to be intimate with women and they wanted unemotional, no-strings attached fun.

Their desire was for our body parts to attach themselves to each other, while making sure the hearts were detached from love.

"You can come over, do your thing and then leave after," are words which often jetted from men's mouths to women's ears, but those words dove into my ears from the mouths of women too.

They would use their winks to close the door behind those words once they settled into my ears.

Crazy to think that the days when I searched for women who would offer nothing much but their body, I thirsted for more.

Days of promiscuity at times, led me to nights where every part of me ached for love, nights I wanted to make love, and caress the soul of a woman who was mine and mine to love forever.

Those days were days when I met women who taught me that double standards were alive and only assumptions and false ideologies were its main source of oxygen.

If the double standard that says men are the only ones who have sex without any attachment whatsoever, then they have not heard the warning shots that women would send right at the start of anything between us.

They would let me know the world has been too cold to them and that they are only searching for a body to warm them up.

I did not turn them down, but I did turn down the cry my ego makes, dying to be fed the exciting parts of those women.

I've had women make me feel guilty, as if I was failing as a man for rejecting sex with them.

I was told that it is a man's job to provide it upon a woman's request, but those same women would turn it down some days when I put in my requests.

When they wanted it, I had to meet their needs. When I needed it, I could only get it if they wanted it. What a concept!

As I continued to silence my ego on my journey of growth, I met some who laughed at me for having a thing going on with celibacy.

Those who knew of my past would think I was crazy for being celibate; others would try to make themselves temptation for me to fall.

I've had men throw dirt on me for chasing the route of purity after a long season of promiscuity. But it was nothing like the women who did not care for my choice to keep myself for my future wife. They wanted a piece of the pie and they needed it right then and there. If I dared to deny, I was a 'no-good punk'.

Yet, I was still believed to be the one who could not resist sex.

Besides the fact that we are believed to be insensitive and without souls by countless women; sometimes we are on the opposite end of the world's standard when it comes to being the hunter/initiator when it comes to the chase or intercourse. Some believe us to be all about sex and good for nothing, but sex and money.

I have seen quite a few broken women who see men in the light that foolish men see them. Those men pledge allegiance to money over girls (of course they use worse language) while some of the women's response prove sex and materialism over love. It's unfortunate that humans sometimes don't see each other as more than an object of pleasure or a source for gain.

Women are sometimes the ones playing men and are being influenced more and more to see things from the angle of promiscuous men. In a generation of moral decline, it seems to be more of a competition between the two. 'You did me wrong', so I am going to let the pain take the pilot seat and do someone of your kind in the way I was done, whether consciously or subconsciously. As people aim to not get feelings involved, with fear of love heavy on their chest, they make sex to be something for pleasure only. It removes the bonding aspect of it, the most important part. This is a habit that is well associated with the male species, however they are no longer the only ones as it seems.

Men are not the only ones demanding meaningless sex. This is the truth that most people can agree that exists, but believe it doesn't really happen because it changes the narrative that says 'men are dogs and women are angels'. I have had times in my life where I felt as if I wasn't man enough or something was wrong with me because I wanted more than just sex. There were times that I craved loved and wanted a bond or intimacy and at times because of that I have been thought to be unmanly.

I have met women who found me attractive, but did not want anything from me but pleasure. Those women would walk in my life the times I would be looking for something serious, something that offers more than the flings I had before. It would bother me that it was all I was worth to them. (*This is one of the things that put in perspective to me what I was doing when I would go after women for more than just sex, getting a taste of my own medicine opened my eyes*).

"You should come over," someone told me once. "You have a man and you know I am not looking for just that," I replied. "It's not like we are making love, it's just sex," she replied to me. She continued talking to me until I caved in. I drove to her house with this belief that if I turned it down, she would see me as a punk. I convinced myself that this would be my opportunity to show her that I was the man, if I could dominate her sexually.

I failed many times; although I wanted to show them I was more and wanted more. I failed at proving that men are not always about sex. "How could you not want sex when a woman is offering?" some men would ask, or "Why did you cave in, you dog?" some women would ask. The truth is that as a man, it's hard to practice self-control. It gets easier as you practice it, but it's not easy to flee from temptation. It is not in our heart to do so and our desires aren't for it, it's like being offered food while fasting. You may not want to eat to reach your goal, but everything in you says, "Food, food, food!" I failed the same way that many women fail when men apply persistency, except I wasn't lured by sweet words, but good promises.

As men, we reach an age where we grow tired of moving from body to body. We grow tired of meaningless flings and abusing our temple as well. Some call it maturity and others call it living the way men ought to be. Regardless of how people title it, some us of strive to be more than souls who chase nothing of substance but all pleasure. Many of us want more and we are condemned for it not only by males, but by women as well.

I can count on more than two hands how many times I've had intercourse simply because I owed someone a favor. "How is that possible?" some might say. Well, I've had women who forced themselves on me and wanted sex from me, instead of saying no and sounding like less than a man, I kept promising that the time would come and eventually the time came. You may say that is foolish, but it's similar to any woman who keeps giving themselves to be loved. Instead, I gave myself to be respected, to be considered 'the man'.

I even allowed this behavior to come in between my relationships, letting women throw themselves at me, rejecting them when it felt necessary, but leaving the door open where they knocked until they got in and I cheated. I cannot blame those women for my decisions nor do I make excuses for my choices, but I am saying that we as men are influenced by the process of manipulation as well and sometimes we let it ruin good things.

There are countless men like me who have seen the tables turn in a way that society doesn't speak about. Men aren't always the ones initiating sex, sometimes they feel as if they have to give it to not feel emasculated or simply because it will put them in good standing with the person they do it with. More than ever, our generation is becoming sexualized and this narrative is being followed by countless men. I will give myself away because society tells me I am a man and I should not refuse sex.

Men have every right as any woman does to treat sex as something valuable. As I practiced celibacy before I tied the knot, it was like seeing a unicorn running around in a field of money to some women when they heard about me abstaining. Some thought it was a lie or asked me how I do it, while others mocked me and thought the notion that a man is saying no to sex is laughable. The unfortunate thing is that there were women who would advocate that their girlfriend stop sleeping with men who aren't willing to love them, yet find me wanting to not give myself to women who aren't going to be my wife, crazy.

Her Insecurities Fed Mine

She asked me, "Who is that girl, do you have history with her?"

I used to be quick to respond with the truth, but now I paused.

If I told her, "Yes," then she might think I was trying to rekindle a fire that once existed.

If I told her, "No," then it would catch up with me later on and stab my relationship where it could bleed to death.

If I decided to say nothing, it would leave room for my silence to be interpreted. Nine times out of ten, the assumptions birthed, would be wrong and that would align with her bad experiences more than the actual truth.

I still try to grasp how telling the truth to her sometimes was adding fuel to the fire, it should have been easy, but she only had eyes to find the worst in every honest thing I had to say.

I admitted to her that the beauty of other women grabbed my attention at times and that I had to fight temptation. Instead of saying, "No I don't," like many lying men did, she would speak to me as if I was the scum of the earth and act like being tempted is only what the weak deal with.

I could argue that even Jesus was tempted on this earth, but was afraid she might whisper some blasphemous things back.

If I expressed things about the relationship I wanted her to work on, because they were slowly abusing my love for her, she would proceed to list every imperfection I had.

If I vented to her, she would interrupt my voice with her own issues, listening to my problems not being something she cared to practice.

She hinted often that she wanted to be understood and everything in me would want to say, "Me too!" But I did not wish to hear about men being more inconsistent in that area.

Unfortunately, I fought with my own demons and the demons in the relationship alone.

I did not tell her when other women approached me; I would fight it off knowing sometimes saying it would have been easier to entertain, when I was expected to do so anyway.

I did not bring up the problems in the relationship any more, I prayed they would go away or just let them live. I hoped they wouldn't become the issue that was swept under the rug, causing our fall.

I did not prioritize honesty anymore; I expressed what I believed she wanted to hear to keep the peace.

I did not tell her about my bad days or the time that life pressed all of its weight on me, instead I listened to her vent and agreed with her about everything.

I have never been a 'Yes man', not to my friends or to anyone, but I grew to say, "Yes ma'am," to her.

I could feel myself being pulled out of the relationship and sometimes I wondered if it was a relationship. It didn't matter; she still defined everything by what it meant to her.

Maybe this is what people call 'happy wife, happy life'. I did not marry her, nor did I ever want to become one of those husbands whose words were just sounds in the air.

I decided to hang on until I had enough. While waiting, I kept on fighting my own demons and hoped one of the lust demons didn't get the best of me.

I had been there before, where I ended up cheating out of misery.

It had not fully reached the point of misery, so perhaps that's why I had not yet built the courage to leave.

A man's insecurities can kill many relationships, but a woman's insecurities can bury some alive. There are relationships where men are dating women who have yet to stop believing that men are the worst things on earth. Usually those women are insecure and nothing a man can do in her eyes will be good. Everything that a man does tends to make women compare a new man with a man they've had before. Subconsciously, they are always ready to catch a man in the wrong whether the man is doing wrong or not. Telling the truth sometimes raises as much doubt as lying to them. It's an 'I will never win' situation with those men.

I've been stuck in relationships before where I felt like I would never see a victory. When I told her things from a realistic standpoint, it got me backlash and honesty became too hard to believe. And, when I said what sounded good it was the same effect. It sounded too good to be true. There are relationships being choked to death right now by a woman who refuses to believe her man is different, pushing him to be like everyone else.

Men in those relationships feel trapped, they feel as if they will never be understood by their woman and will always be serving the wrath of her brokenness. Those men become filled with frustration and time with their friends becomes more precious than being with their women because they always anticipate arguments and expect to lose. They never communicate what they feel and never reach true intimacy with their women.

Unfortunately, many of the men in such situations do not leave, instead they find someone else while maintaining their relationship. No, not every man has the guts to walk away, instead they try to hold on to the relationship while searching for happiness outside of it. Others grow to believe that it is 'just a woman being a woman' and will do whatever to walk the line and to keep his woman happy enough since he believes any other woman he picks will have similar characteristics.

As a man, I always want to share the deep things with my partner. I want her to know the good, bad and ugly and not feel judged or marked for it. I don't want my faults and my past used against me. I once believed that women do not want two things from me: the truth or being told what to do. Though I do believe the tone in which men say things makes a big difference; we fail to pay attention to our tone. But, we shouldn't have to play conversations in our head making sure they are something our women will not blow up about. Men are tired of women treating them as their exes. It's a crying shame when a woman doesn't want to talk about her past because she doesn't want to give off the wrong ideas about her. When a man is courageous enough to tell her about his past, it is often used as ammo to kill the relationship. It's so unfair when a woman says to be honest, yet she overreacts to it or grows angry when compared to his ex. Yet, men are regularly graded and evaluated based on a woman's ex.

A woman's insecurity can be deadly and life altering for a man. It has turned some men cold and men are being blamed for it. It's not always a man's fault, his best sometimes is not good enough for his woman or the women he has been with.

Men want to be understood, as well as women. Not enough women realize that. Many women waste their time blocking out our cries with their complaints, comparing us in the light of their previous partners, instead of learning more about us. Then they condemn us for becoming mutes whom they can't figure us out.

We've been pressured enough by society to hide our feelings, but it only causes us to do worse when we do try to open up to a woman and she's too self-centered to listen. Or too insecure to hear our desire to heal with her and too busy reliving her past to see our good intentions.

I Am Not For Keeping

I overheard her and her friends talking over the phone once.

They sounded like daughters of Einstein, trying to solve the world's most difficult problem.

Her friend uttered, "I wish I knew how to get into his head. Maybe that's how I'll be able to finally keep a man."

My facial expression became that of a perplexed individual; I could not see why getting into a man's head would be the goal of a woman, if the man isn't opening his mind to her.

They make it out to be science when it's as simple as basic math.

1+1 = 2. Add a man who wants to be in a relationship + a woman who wants to be in a relationship = a good couple.

I kept the words trapped under my tongue and said nothing instead of yelling, "Maybe you can't keep them because you keep picking the wrong kind or you're not worth staying with," loudly enough for her girl friend to hear.

The truth hurts and offends, but sometimes it's all about the timing.

As my woman got off the phone, I said, "I am here not because you are practicing some formula that keeps me here, it is because I want to. It's because I want to be with you."

It was random to her and she did not see the point of me saying this and instead took it as me giving her a beautiful compliment as I sometimes did.

Though I wanted to explain myself, I did not. I continued to be a man consistent with effort and loving with his actions, in hopes that it could give her enough wisdom to share with her girlfriend.

Women must understand that the secret to keeping a man is to find a man who wants to keep them. A man will make keeping you and keeping you happy, a priority. I've seen far too many women pick a man and demand that he stay when he doesn't want to. Instead of walking away, they hold on tighter trying to get a better grip, stabbing their own heart while trying to make a man become what he doesn't want to be, the man for them.

Nothing makes my ear bleed more than hearing women complain about how men do not live up to par to what they ought to be in a relationship. Often times, those men simply don't want to be in a relationship. It's like trying to get a caterpillar to be a butterfly before its time. They are not ready to take that step and are also unwilling.

I've been the man a few women have tried to keep. I watched them do things, such as keep up with their looks, put me on a pedestal, prioritize my needs and go to desperate measures for me. All of this in hopes that I would stay around and give my heart. I stayed around, but never gave them my heart. I didn't want to give my heart to them nor could I be convinced to.

Still, I let them believe that it was possible. I accepted their love, and all they were willing to give me and gave them nothing back in return. There is nothing I hate more as a grown man, than people telling me what to do. These women did not directly tell me what to do, but they used their actions to speak it, doing whatever they believed necessary to convince me to love them. They failed and only broke their own hearts. It wasn't me looking to manipulate or use them. It was me being with those women without any real conditions or purpose. Those relationships to me were just relationships I got myself into with no real intentions and made sure it stayed that way.

Keeping a man should never be a woman's job. Keeping anyone should never be anyone's job - period. We must learn to keep relationships as simplified things; instead, we complicate them too much. There are even relationships with a complicated status, which to me doesn't make much sense. Either you are in a relationship or you're not. If it's consistently not working, there is a hint that it may not be it.

Quite often, we try to force things that aren't meant to be. We see that there is a dead end up ahead, yet we try to pave a road because we want to journey with that person. Relationships are about two people in love, not one in love while the other is trying to figure out what they want. Nor is it about one holding on to their single ways, while the other is trying to find out how to keep the relationship steady.

A woman displaying love with action, spoiling her man, and making sure he is happy and well taken care of will not make that man love her. A man, who cares for her, will see those things as beautiful gifts and will lead to him loving her more, but it will not be enough to convince a man who doesn't want a relationship, to build with her.

Nothing, absolutely nothing, can keep a man who doesn't want to be kept. Nothing will make a man who doesn't want to be in love, fall in love with a woman. Everything that has to do with dating, relationships and love, must be mutual, consensual and natural. Anything forced will not last.

I beg you not to beg anyone to love you.

The fastest way to lose yourself is to try to find love in a soul that doesn't have it for you. That is digging the hole you will bury your own heart in.

Love is a gift that ought to be given freely, but if they aren't giving it, do not try to suck it out of them.

In this world, many pains are self-inflicted, people getting burned by the fire they were playing with. I pray you never become one of those who plan their own heartache.

- Unborn Daughter

Black Rose

Beautiful, but black.

Bad, because black is a representation of evil and a bad fruit I am believed to be, because my melanin is the spouse of darkness.

Every time I walk through detectors, fear creeps within me, hoping nothing goes off and my innocence will not be enough to prove that I'm not guilty.

Every late night run I've had, I had to make sure to position myself where it's obvious that I'm not in attack mode, nor am I escaping from anything.

Every time I'm in an area where stereotypes say I don't belong, I allow my silence to hint to people that I'm aware, but let my actions whisper that I am uncomfortable. I will make myself comfortable to make your prejudiced mind uncomfortable.

I often question the praise I've received for my accomplishments, wondering if I would be praised if I wasn't black and if the odds weren't so stacked against me.

I became best friends with a pessimist mindset as fuel to reach my dreams. "I'm expected to fail so why not try, can it count against me?" I subconsciously ask myself.

Sometimes I comically say, "It is because I'm black," to help alleviate the guilt of those who mistreat me because of my melanin.

I find safety in mixed women because they satisfy my desire to be with my own race, yet fulfill my desire to date freely outside of my own race.

I experience limited freedom, something hard to understand by those who've never been scolded by both races for dating outside those races.

I try to do 'non-black things', so I don't become the typical black guy in the eyes of all races. Yet those things alienate me from the black people who feel that they don't fit the stereotype enough.

I feel obligated to cooperate with authorities just as much as I feel obligated to cooperate with the 'real niggas' I bump into in a place where I don't belong, yet people believe I call home. I fear either one of them might harm me for the wrong reasons.

I am 'too white' to some of the black people I know because of my speech and intelligence and 'too black' to some of the white people I know because of my skin, my loud music and athletic abilities.

"You're not black", I hear from those of other races who see the content of my heart. "You're not all that, not better than us", I hear from those of the same race who see the results of my labor.

Every day I am supposed to compete to be loved and accepted, fighting a war not because of who I am, but the color I am and am not.

To any race, I am sometimes a fantasy, idol, inspiration, and example. But to many, I am what my skin labels me to be.

I am the Black Rose, different from the rest, yet questioned in my environment.

I did not grow from the concrete; I grew from a field of everything.

I have accepted that in this field there are cliques, stereotypes, and there are many things that should not grow there.

I will never wish that I was planted elsewhere, but I will search for the one who provide the soil, the water and the sunlight and find why he planted me here. And I will do just that until I am completely withered.

I am a Black Rose; I am not meant to be like all the others, but to live differently whether I am appreciated or disliked for what I look like.

I do not know if they seek revenge or if they seek equality.

The lines seem to be smeared.

On some days, I want to stand by them and support what they say their focus is. I'm human just as a woman is and to see a woman treated fairly would only be human nature for anyone one with a beating heart, although it isn't.

On other days, I stand away from them, watching them foolishly rip the male species apart in their speech and attempt to take anything good a man can offer on this earth.

It's quite disturbing that many women seem to fight for equality by bullying men, making us out to be less.

I don't know if they realize that they are doing to good men what terrible men have done to them, but I do know the smell of anger is strong on their breaths, their bodies reeking of resentment.

This world seems to thrive on 'an eye for an eye'. I guess that's what blind people do.

If anything, I hope they see that all men aren't the same as they believe them to be and that all men aren't comfortable with what men before us did.

I know it's a hard world for women, but I surely hope that they don't believe the world will become easier with men by making it harder on men.

- Femi-Nazi

The *Healing*

Growth

I was having a conversation with a friend of mine.

He said: "Things have changed", I nodded in agreement to this general fact.

The world has had a lot of transformations since we were kids. It's the obvious.

He then put the microscope on his statement and continued saying, "The guys who never used to get the girls, seem to be getting them. Being popular and eye candy isn't working out as good bait anymore," narrowing down his conversation to dating.

I replied, "Maybe some women are tired of those types of men once they are out of their teens. Maybe their hearts have suffered enough." Hinting that we are much older and dating and love has new meanings.

He paused and whispered, "*Hmmm*, maybe."

As he digested the thought, I spoke again, adding more, "However, I do believe many women chase the superficiality still. There are plenty of women in this world who act as if physical strength will compensate for emotional and mental weakness. They believe swag is an acceptable representation of financial security and that material items define a man."

He paused once again, as if the thought landed in the blood flow to his brain and was traveling its way through every corner of his mind.

"I mean...." he attempted to respond, but seeing that he did yet to know what to say, I interrupted.

"Or maybe you've been after different types of women now, mature women who desire more," I said.

I have been around him for a fair amount of my life, I've seen his athleticism, and popularity and smooth words grab any girl while we were younger.

Besides, he once won over the heart of the first girl I ever fell for to prove a point to me, to prove that being a good guy wasn't the secret ingredient to winning hearts.

He was new to the dating scene once again after taking a hiatus to focus on far more important things in his life and now he was back. And now men like me seem to have the upper hand.

"Back in the day, dudes who never used to get the bad ones are now getting the bad ones," he said, hinting that things had changed for me.

According to him, quality women seem to be gravitating to me and though he may connect with some attractive ones, he has yet to land on one mature and God fearing enough. One with a total package, in shape physically and mentally, as well as spiritually.

"I don't know, I've been fortunate I guess," I replied. "I don't look at body first, although it is important. I don't care for the bad ones, I care for the mature ones and I guess some happen to be bad," I answered to him.

"I meet the bad ones, but after having conversations with them, I lose interest. I want a woman who keeps her body right but when I find one, there's no mental connection with her or we're not on the same level," he responded as soon as I finished my last word.

"Maybe what you want now can't be found by how you've always searched for them," I ended the conversation.

Maturing and desiring more quality partners and meaningful relationships is not a thing only women do. Those of us (males) who are growing into men, we too desire substance. You would be speaking a level of truth if you said, "Many men, all they care about is finding a woman who looks good, with a nice chest and behind," but too many women let that truth infiltrate their minds as the idea that 'all men' are this way.

I was once a man too shallow for love. I searched for the woman with the big booty and coke bottle shaped body. Which is what was the norm, as well as what the hip hop culture promoted as the ideal woman, along with a fetish for beautiful Hispanic women. I did not care for a while for the type of woman you were. I was part of the demographic of guys who did not care for the woman's heart, but rather her appearance.

Whether she was a champion or not didn't matter, as long she was jewelry on my arm that was all that mattered to me. I did not notice how flawed this belief was until I begin to separate myself from the norm, through maturing and lots of renewing of my mind through the word of God. What I considered a 'ride or die' chick or a 'wifey type', was full of fallacy and having one of those types, alone were childish goals.

The more I grew, the more I craved substance, the more my search for women transitioned into searching for one woman. The more my preference changed from wanting a 'bad chick', to wanting a good woman who was good looking enough.

As my perspective changed, the type of people I attracted also changed. I wanted a wife, I was not going to entertain anyone who did not have such potential. When those who weren't wife material according to my standards came along, I walked away. I didn't want to waste my time nor give women who didn't have much to offer, the attention to make them believe that I was okay with who they were. I did not want to show any support of their ways because I also knew how negatively it affected some women. More than enough times, the women I was interested in found it to be rare that I enjoyed being single and hard to believe that I wouldn't entertain the 'bad chicks'. I noticed there was envy in the hearts of some and insecurity resting in lives of many.

Although those women had great personalities, beautiful and everything a good matured man would want, they compared their luck to the success the bad chicks had. They looked at the amount of men who were interested, the amount of them who followed through compared to the number of men who actually are lured to the 'bad chicks'.

They couldn't understand that although they did have a lot of men flocking to them, it did not mean that they were attracting good men. They weren't attracting the kind of men who would love them and be willing to build with them. In the pool of those men, were a lot of boys fishing for a woman to stroke their egos, fulfilling their fantasies. The fact that no women were in my DMs, I didn't have a bunch of texting buddies and so forth, surprised the women interested in me. I did not try to make them believe me, but reminded them that people attract what they are and what they desire deep down. My desires and focus changed from the immature, 'wanna-be mac daddy', I used to be. Craving vixens was a thing of the past for me, wanting the best looking woman for show was dead to me. Seeking a mate based on attraction was foolish to me.

I attracted quality women because I changed and my needs and wants changed also. If anything, I tried to convince my male friends that I have lived more now that my desires changed as maturity does its work. Things were different for my buddy because he was becoming someone different. His search was based on who he was in the past, while trying to find a woman for who he was becoming. There will always be a conflict until the two align.

To have a woman who is the right package, a man must have his mind, spirit and his eyes right. I kept reiterating to him that the 'bad ones' that I had were not because I was looking at them physically, but because they were beautiful inside. Not only that they searched for something different, but because they wanted substance and quality too, so we connected. They weren't after attention; they wanted love - true love.

There will always be males who chase girls like hormonal teens. There will also be those who refuse to be men; there will always be girls who concentrate on being eye candy and a man's jewelry more than they are actually looking for a quality man to love and grow with. To find someone of substance, you yourself must be someone of substance. The more a man grows, the more his desire changes, his preferences will just not remain the same. Women who do not offer much nor do they truly desire much are out there and are being won over by crappy men. It's what they are after. To want different and more, you must be different and more.

It is necessary to understand that simply wanting love does not mean you're ready for it.

Your immature desires and shallow needs do not disqualify you for love, but votes you out in terms of being ready for it. To meet a quality partner and find true love, your mindset must be on that.

You cannot be holding on to your childish ways, while begging to have what grandma and grandpa had. That is for grown folks.

Natural

She thinks her stretch marks are unattractive, yet I've never truly paid attention to them.

She thinks she doesn't look good without make up, yet this is the face I fall asleep to and wake up to; it's the face I love.

She believes the little weight she has gained makes her ugly, yet it never stopped me from loving her.

She believes without the long hair or certain things done to it that her head is hideous, yet to me the styles are all the same.

I do not know why she tries to uphold these standards, perhaps she is competing with the beauty-enhanced models or the media.

Whichever one it is, I can say that a man, who loves her, will love the raw and natural version of her.

The men, who told her the natural things about her aren't enough, are boys still chasing fantasies and who aren't able to love what is real.

I am not that man.

I love her just the way she is, some things about her may not be my favorite things, but never will they keep me from loving her.

If anything I want her to be, herself, down to every part of her.

There are many things about women that women cannot appreciate about themselves that men truly do not care about. As a man, things that are problems to women, such as stretch marks, natural beauty, uneven breasts, and cellulite have never bothered me. Neither have I met many men who refused to be with a woman who he deeply cares for simply because something natural about her turned him off.

A man who isn't in love with a woman will always find reasons and things not to like about her. When someone isn't your favorite person, it is easy to put a magnifying glass on the smallest thing and make it bigger and uglier than it is. I've grown to believe that there are things that women simply hate about themselves, but blame men for it.

A woman's weight may bother a man a bit, it's normal because nobody wants a partner who lets themselves go, but never in my lifetime have I seen it to be enough for them to put an end to a beautiful relationship. Only in relationships that were already heading downhill. I've been a fitness freak before and have had standards that I wanted to be met, but never did I tell myself I would not bend them.

I began to hate the weight one of my previous partners had gained and left the relationship, but the weight was never truly the issue, but because I started comparing too much. They say, "Comparison is the thief of joy," and it really is. I left this ex under those conditions because I was comparing her to other women, such as the fitness models.

It started as an innocent thing, me looking at fit women to suggest to her; then I began to lust after those women, building fantasies about them, spending too much time looking at their

Instagram pages. Then I started growing angry that my woman did not have desires like this or have a body like that. That became enough for me to say that it was over.

Our relationship was already under the fire and that was fuel to burn it down. It was never about her weight, but about lust catching my eyes and winning my heart. After I lost her, she went on to gain more weight and that didn't stop me one bit when I tried to win her back. I cared for her during those times and wanted to be with her so her weight became irrelevant.

Makeup on a woman is something as a man I never cared much for, with or without it, if I was with that woman it was because I was attracted to her both inside and out. Many men appreciate its enhancements from far away, when they see women out and about. But I have met very few who appreciate it to the same level when the woman is close to them, when she is theirs. It doesn't make or break anything for a man if they are with the woman.

There are men who make a big deal about it simply in the pursuing stages, unrealistic expectations had them believe that a woman's face is as smooth and perfectly blended as when he saw her out and about. Loving a woman to me has always been about loving her for who she truly is, which means with, makeup or no makeup. If you're with a woman, you will have to see her without makeup, if you marry that woman, you'll get the naked face more than the makeup. How can you fall in love with anything besides her natural beauty?

I've had more trouble with makeup on a woman than without it, like many men I hate that it smears on our face and clothes; I hate that it takes so long, I hate that it costs so much. I accept it on my woman, but never has it become a barrier between our love.

Things about a woman's body that are completely normal and natural imperfections, truly do not affect most men. Unlike weight and makeup, they have very to no little effect at all. I have yet to hear a man speak on those things. They are things women look upon and talk about, that we pay very little attention to. It has never stopped a man from doing anything with or for a woman. I am not saying there aren't shallow men who do not see past these things, but I have never met a man in love who pays attention to them.

When anger fills the air and sarcasm floats its way into the atmosphere, she finds subtle ways to voice her requests.

She acts as a serpent trying to catch its prey, wisely maneuvering herself until she can strike with the right words.

"You're okay baby?" she would ask. Based on the tone of my reply and the speed of it out of my mouth, she would either get closer or widen the gap of space.

Sometimes I am as unsure as she is as whether to approach me or not.

However, she knows me better than myself and quite often handles things better than I.

Alas, I've met a woman who understands my anger is short-lived, I'll be fine after, unless she continues to ask me if I'm okay and proceed to tell me that I don't look as if I am.

She knows that my sarcasm is a defense mechanism and that when my emotions are calm, an apology will find its way to her.

She has learned that the stress will never take me, so when it comes to grab me hostage, I will shortly free myself. When the calm comes, it will clear the air for her to encourage me.

I'm fortunate to say it is finally time that I've met a woman who understands that men are different, and when we go through things, it's hard to talk about it because our mind is busy trying to find solutions.

I know to communicate but I never want questions to remind me of my current state or interrupt my thinking as I come up with a master plan I may or may not follow.

- Anger

Misinterpreting My Silence

She thinks I'm mad, but I am far from it.

My mind is so far from thinking about our daily routines such as talking a little, joking a little, or messing around a little.

Today the cares of the world are what's running through my mind, not her, not us.

I am in this math class called life, trying to solve some of the problems that she has yet to open the book to see.

She isn't ignorant nor is she careless, but she is simply not as knowledgeable about the burden I carry on my shoulders at times.

I stare at the bills and hear them violently screaming at me, demanding what I owe them, yet my wallet begs for more time.

My career is beautiful, but there are ugly sides to it and when I look at the ugly side it terrifies me, it irks me and discourages me.

Sometimes I feel that I am not being the best I am supposed to be, I hear failure whisper, "You are my son," and I listen to him.

Fear jumps in while I wrestle with doubt and throws a few punches.

Depression has been trying to enter this door for a while, it made its way in one night, but I doubled up my security through prayer and now it sits outside waiting for an opportunity, like a mean dog barking loudly and sometimes like a patient wolf.

Regret from time to time visits me to tell me terrible stories about my past and to try to convince me that I am no good.

World War III is taking place inside of my mind and all I can do is try to silence it.

Peace is what I am after and tears I am trying to keep from making their way to my eyes.

I am not mad, but I am not okay and I do not know how to communicate this stuff.

I've gotten better with you than I was with my previous partners, but there's still a blockage in my throat.

I am not mad, but I am looking for some space to turn the voice of regret and fear off and regain control.

You are not the burden, I am not growing to no longer desire you, our relationship isn't on shaky grounds.

I am trying to make some good lemonade out of the lemons that life is throwing at me, and right at this moment the lemons are hitting me and it hurts.

Don't misinterpret my silence, attempt to learn it instead of assuming.

Besides, you've begged me to learn yours.

Silence can mean a million things to different people; its meaning is very subjective. The women I've been with are often silent because they are thinking about what to say when they are angry or simply because they are angry. Many of the women I have met and observed use silence to overthink things and make matters of their relationships worse when they speak. I have yet to meet a woman whose silence can be interpreted as a time of peace or in the same manner as it is to me. I am sure that they exist, but I have yet to meet them.

Maybe I've been unlucky, but the fact still remains that I have known silence to be a woman's calm before the storm. Perhaps it is why the ones I have been with thought negatively when I was silent; because it was the message that their silence often represented. However, it was always far from that. My silence has always freed me from the thoughts of the world or the thoughts of the world haven't let my mind be free. I am silent when I am trying to figure out something, when I am thinking of a plan and even when I am thinking of nothing. Most likely there is nothing wrong with the relationship that's torturing my mind, but there is something wrong either with me or something going wrong for me.

Men on average talk a lot less than women, whether men are with their woman, their friends or by themselves, it's proven that on average men say less than women. I can ride in the car all day with one of my boys and we share just a few words, and that's okay and far from being awkward. I've never been able to do so with the women I've been with in my past; it would raise a red flag for them if my lips did not say anything to them and would cause many of them to start an investigation in their head.

Nothing caused me to grow irritated more than being asked, "Are you okay?" numerous times when I was okay and I just did not desire to utter a word. That phrase would be the exact words they used to break the ice that freezes the silence of the moment. Then they would ask "What's wrong? Is it me?" They would shoot different questions at me trying to figure me out when I just did not desire to speak. I would repeat, "Nothing", numerous times until I grew too annoyed to even share with them.

Unfortunately, nothing would ever give those women a reason to stop. They would play guessing games in their heads and come up with their own conclusions. To some women, my silence meant guilt was trapped in my throat. They would assume that I was cheating and have no words to say to them because I was somehow in the wrong. To other women, it would mean that I was unsatisfied with them. They would see my silence as a way for me to voice my loss of interest. Some of them saw it as me planning on how to let the relationship down easy and the few I deeply loved would assume that I was angry or mad about something in the relationship.

I am no different than numerous fellas on this earth; my silence has gotten misinterpreted and has caused women to come up with conclusions that have only caused more issues in our relationship, issues that should have never existed.

We, as men, often refrain from breaking our silence simply because it's hard for us. We don't see how talking about our issues will solve anything when there's indeed a problem right in our face. We do not like to hear ourselves talk about our problems because we want solutions, a fair amount of us do not like pity parties.

We may not want anyone in our business but ourselves, and many of us have been taught that we must shut up or man up about our problems, which is usually the best solution that comes to mind at times. We know that it would be better to communicate our feelings and be logical adults about it, but many times we want to, but out of habit it's hard for us.

In many cases we want to do so on our own timing, which is much later when we've figured things out, it calms our mind down. No different than the woman who can't stop herself from thinking the worst when her man is being mute, we don't know how to communicate our feelings, or at least in a timely fashion.

Don't think badly of our silence unless we give you reason to. Until you stop nagging us about opening up, we probably won't, but we will instead give more of the silent treatment. Bear with us, some of us grow out of it, but it's not easy.

I Said "It" First

I have heard that words can be so heavy on the soul that they can weigh down the mind until they are spat out.

But for me, the only weight I felt was the weight on my tongue.

My mouth struggled to open, and as my lips trembled I felt my tongue sweating out saliva that is supposed to help me swallow my pride.

But it wasn't that simple, I've held on to these words countless times, giving room for my partner to say it first, which I believed would give me the upper hand.

I could easily let my pride coach me out of doing what I needed to do, which was to dive head first.

My heart raced, doing its own cardio, attempting to outperform the fear running through my veins.

There was war going on within me. The young and immature me was choking the older and far more mature me. They are enemies, two brothers I find hard to discipline at times.

The young me continued to get a tighter grip, blocking the words from finding their way out of my voice box.

It wanted me to follow the norm and wash those words down with alcohol, and paint over them with careless actions.

"I can't and I won't," kept going back and forth in my thoughts, battling with, "I want to and I should," like a tennis match.

Perhaps it is because I understood the importance of those words, maybe they fully described what I had longed for deep down, but had yet to find.

Maybe it's because I've heard them used before by those who wanted me to believe that they were here to stay, but never stayed long enough to confirm the meaning.

Maybe when I say it, I would mean it, therefore every letter became bricks on my tongue that refused to excuse themselves without force.

"I love you," I said to her finally silencing the war in my mind.

I heard myself say it and a bit of the weight of uncertainty came off of my shoulder.

Although doubts tried to convince me that I did not mean what I said to her, deep down those words had been living in me, dying to come out.

They had been watered by my heart and grown roots deep in my soul. It was so evident that I loved her, but my mind had known no good experience with love, so its best advice was to tell me not to listen to any part of me.

It could not convince me to keep it inside and never let it out, but now I would have to keep myself from regretting it.

Whoever says, "I love you," first in a relationship should not matter. How they respond when you first say it should mean something, but it shouldn't define the entire relationship, however in many cases it does.

For years, I felt that whoever said, "I love you," first in the relationship took the lower position of the relationship, the loser's position. I did not always believe so. The first time I wanted to say I love you to someone, I didn't have much resistance. My heart raced and the thought made me happy with very little hesitancy.

Beyond my first relationship, it became harder. Not because I did not truly feel an amount of love for any of my partners that came after, but because I've watched those words get tossed to the side while my relationship goes down the drain. The few times that I uttered, "I love you," I did not hold on to the meaning in enough of my relationships. Insecurities and tough times overrode every good thing those words attached themselves to between me and my exes. Those words became like an empty glass to me, fragile yet empty. The times I felt compelled to say it, I held on to it, waiting for my partner to break and say it first, instead of letting it fly out of my heart through my mouth like a bird who is no longer caged.

Relationships to me for a while were about competition and I needed the upper hand. Whoever said I love you first was translated into, "I am emotionally at your mercy now. I surrender control to you," type of a deal. I did not misuse the word to manipulate or carry out agendas with wrong intentions, but I used it wisely, on my own terms.

I've always been someone who picked my relationships wisely, I never jumped from relationship to relationship nor did I pick my partner without serious evaluation. Every time I started dating someone, it was after I had learned enough of the lessons from my previous relationship. Therefore when I had a chance to share an 'I love you' with a partner, there were enough credentials behind it. It was never based on my head being in the clouds or without much consideration.

I will say some of the times I said those three words, it was encouraged by sex and lust, but wasn't always the determining factor. Those relationships may not have been true love, but they fit the idea of what love was to me at the time. I can no longer say that the loves I've had before weren't real to me because they were, at that time, my reality. The love wasn't mature or maybe even true love, but love was shown through emotions rather than infatuation.

"I think I am in love with you," followed by, "I think I love you," was the way I heard it said from a woman I was in a short, but very physical relationship with. I said the same words back to her, but did not feel them. I got used to saying them in the middle of having intercourse. I had always heard that when you love someone, sex is the way to bond with them, but it was our sexual bonding that made me believe I was in love. I now consider that love to be only emotions without a true understanding of love.

When she said it back to me, my heart felt safe. She hinted at it way before I did which to me meant that if she left me, at least I wasn't the one who fell in love first. There were two things I knew that put me in the position where I had power over her: getting her virginity and her saying, "I love you," first.

It was what I was taught by older boys as a teen that I would forever be in control if I was the one to get her virginity or if she said she loved me first.

The next time I was in the situation where I heard those words, it was different with better circumstances. She called me and said there was something she needed to say to me. I didn't think anything of it. When we met face to face she was nervous and after a lot of walking in a circle, she grabbed my hands and said, "Alex, I love you." I was surprised because those same feelings were boiling in me the same week. I didn't say anything, not because I feared being first, but I felt it was too early in the relationship. I placed an imaginary mark in my head to when it was acceptable or not to utter those words.

I replied, "I love you too. The other day I was looking at you and said to myself, I'm going to marry that woman." She was surprised and said, "Like wow! We've been thinking the same thing, but neither of us wanted to say it." We both felt relieved, it was more real to me this time around because physicality wasn't the basis of the relationship.

The next time I found myself in this position in a relationship was with my wife. I graduated from holding the 'I love you' in for the purpose of being second and relieving myself of the fear of control. I had adopted a new mindset by then, it was not only to say 'I love you' but to focus on a building a solid relationship. If those three words later became something of no meaning or meaning with bad memories, I promised myself to refrain from seeing it as vanity.

The opportunity presented itself when she called me upset about a minor thing, it confirmed to me that she cared far more than I recognized. After months of dating, the urge was there. I was sure I would be marrying this woman. but timing was all that was left. "I love you," I said on the phone with her, after I calmed her down and explained myself about the situation. It was heavy on my chest; I decided to not resist this time. It was over the phone due to the fact that we were in a long distance relationship, but I could feel the relief her heart felt at that moment.

It happened that she was indeed growing in love with me and became upset because she was starting to care too much and was unsure if I was in the same emotional place too. My reaction to something she said which led to that conversation was nothing bad, but it was upsetting to her because it was not what she wanted to hear from me. That reaction coupled with the thought that the relationship may not be as serious for me, created an issue in her mind. Hearing me say those words came as a relief for her. Growing out of my bad experiences and being willing to risk my heart made it the perfect moment for her as she said, "I love you too." Hanging up the phone, we both felt great joy and felt secure in our relationship.

It's equally as hard for men to say, 'I love you' as it is for women. Some are held back by the fear of being controlled or believing the false ideology that love is a game and whoever says it first loses. However, many have the fear of being rejected. To hear your partner say something that meaningful first, can sometimes be the safety needed to reveal their heart.

Unlike women, lots of men don't feel bubbly emotions and great excitement when they are ready to say it. Many times for men, it is more nervousness and fear. Men seem to be more afraid and unwilling to take the love risk than women, which results in many more women expressing their love words first. Saying it and meaning it, that is. Countless men say these words freely with bad intentions, using it as a key to get what they want. But those who mean it want it to mean something when said, which is why there's so much resistance in the act of saying it.

I Waited for Her

I am not a perfect saint, but I am being perfected and in that process I aim to do everything God's way.

When we met, there was a spark, a shock to my system.

The conversation was flowing, the similarities kept introducing themselves as we spoke and we were engaged in each other's presence.

The more we discovered about each other, the more fuel was being added to our physical attraction.

The desire to connect physically was there, but it could only visit my thoughts, and had no invitation to stay.

I had grown too much spiritually to go back to my carnal ways, but that did not mean that my carnal ways did not want to take precedence over my spiritual life.

"I will wait, I can wait for her, it's the right thing to do," I would tell myself. My heart would agree, but my mind would start a debate.

"You are a man and men do not wait, they are the lions of the jungle; they must mark their territory and prove themselves in the bedroom. Besides, you must test it out before you make it officially yours. We aren't made to be monogamous," would be conversations going on in my thoughts as a rebuttal to what my heart desired.

There was war inside of me, but there was also joy. For, I desired to love a human being beyond sex. Sex had controlled me far too much in the past and made me believe that lust is love on too many occasions.

The times we were in each other's presence while in a relationship, felt like a beautiful maze also filled with landmines. Almost everything she did made me thirst for a physical connection more.

A man who is able to control himself is a wise man, I would tell myself. "Prove to sex that you will not let it lead all of your relationship," I would challenge myself.

Days and hours went on and we held on.

Held on to the belief that sex is for marriage. Intercourse can wait.

We fell in love with each other's personality and sense of humor. Our heart grew closer to love, with love truly being the glue.

We built our friendship and communicated more than I ever had with anyone. Our relationship took a route I had never known before, for it was the first time I truly knew the person I was falling in love with. No one could convince me that it wasn't real because it had no outside source affecting it, but love.

And on my wedding day, I became far more grateful for doing it God's way.

The woman who was walking down the aisle was a woman I treated completely different than any woman I had been with. I knew this woman, I knew the deep things of her, and I loved her without a clouded vision.

As tears dripped from eyes, I admired her beauty from the perspective of purity. I said to myself, "I thank God I waited."

I waited for her.

7 had been a celibate man for quite some time, but before I became a married man, I had fallen and gotten up a couple of times. Those were the tougher days of my life because it seemed as if hypocrisy was settling in my heart, although I did not walk into sex without guilt, but fell into temptation. I was very proud of where I was in my Christian walk and had been a solid man of faith. Somehow I forgot that we all can fall short if we aren't guarded and lose our focus on Christ.

I lost focus, chasing other things and divorcing myself from my prayer life. I wasn't drawing strength from my spiritual life at all which made it a bit easier to be pulled in by a couple of old habits. When I entered relationships while walking with God, being celibate became something easy to talk about but still hard to live by. It had to be done.

Falling was not a reason to stay down and revert back to living as if sex was nothing but pleasure; but rather a gift from God that should be used how God intended for it to be used. Dating and waiting until marriage seemed to be something abnormal in this generation, yet I did not let that dictate how I lived my life. I focused on operating with the mindset that living pure is normal. A focus that was once foolish to me, became the only lifestyle I knew to be true.

When I first met my wife, we established that we were waiting for marriage. We both had a past where sex controlled most of our relationships and most of our lives like many in this age. Many of the 'I love yous' we uttered in the past were influenced by hormones leading many of those relationships to last longer than they were supposed to because of lust.

We wanted to do things differently from our way and from how this generation believed to be the way. We talked about the benefits of waiting from the non-spiritual sides first since we knew from the spiritual perspective it was mandated. We also talked about the pros and cons of not having the physical included. Things like how our love for each other would not be diluted and how practicing self-control and discipline would help our marriage later on. We also discussed how a strong friendship would grow from all of this. We made it a goal and were willing to do anything to execute it while making God proud.

I wanted to prove to her that there was a man who was willing to wait for her and she wanted to stick to the belief that she was worth the wait.

Unfortunately, we did not discuss all of the difficulties of this. We did not discuss how we had fallen short before and how it gets harder and harder. It's easy to start off with a great plan, but it's not always easy to execute all the way through. In a world where everyone is having sex and it's being promoted heavily outside of marriage, our hormones became a pain in the butt. We both had the right goals and were tired of falling short, yet lust did not care one bit about our plans.

I would kiss her and my thoughts would try to take me other places. Anytime we were alone the intentions started to float in my head. Walking this journey became akin to walking on fire barefooted. It became tough. I decided that it was best to apply wisdom.

A lot of the times we failed, simply because we entertained the temptation too long, which I noticed was the cause for me failing before. Many times instead of walking away and saying no immediately, I played with the thoughts of going further. I wrestled with the possibilities and I pushed myself to believe that if I confront the temptation and fail, it's because I am not strong enough.

For me, being strong enough, meant to withstand in the heat of the situation without folding. I grew to realize that I was wrong. I started trying to do everything with caution. I had to remodel my dating guidelines and rules. We could not date like everyone else, there had to be boundaries and limit. We chose to not hang out in private places together for too long, we did not kiss a certain way or for long period of time, we didn't do certain activities or say certain things. We monitored ourselves to give no room for anything to come in.

The freedom we once had when we dated before seemed to be compromised. I heard before that 'discipline is learning how to delay pleasure' and disciplining ourselves taught me just that. It was difficult, but it helped us in ways we couldn't imagine. I grew to love her for exactly who she was, something many say, but won't back it up if sex isn't present.

We communicated about everything and knew everything about each other, it was the first time I actually knew my woman. We made great progress in terms of handling arguments, there was no make-up love that could put Band-Aids on the arguments; we handled the disagreements and other things as two adults without clouded visions. On our wedding night, it was such a beautiful thing to know that I waited, not only because I loved her, but because I loved God which resulted in me loving her more.

The journey of waiting for a woman is not one many men want to travel, but the idea that it's impossible and unrealistic is biased. It fulfills this idea that men are moved by sex only and that they can never practice self-control. Most people don't see why they should wait for marriage. The majority of those people do not have enough self-control to make that happen. It's not just a man thing.

It's a human thing, we want what we want when we want it. To deny ourselves of anything that is pleasure is self-hate to us, when in reality it is actually loving ourselves on a mature level.

Men are capable of doing it, I did it. There are men out there who will do it for a woman they love. There are men out there who are practicing celibacy. There are men out there who do not want to be with many women or let sex lead him to a lawless path.

As a man who lived the promiscuous life, I never thought I'd ever become one who would wait for one woman. A few of my college friends laughed when they heard I was practicing celibacy, a few people giggled when I told them I was in a relationship but waiting.

Despite who I was and who people believed me to be, I grew up, I changed. I do not believe I would have been able to do it without a spiritual life. There are other men who have not been too indoctrinated by society, who will wait for the woman they believe to be their prize.

Waiting doesn't make you more of a man, but it pushes you to new levels as a man. I could write, "Real Men Wait" but I could never agree with it fully. There are many great men who did not wait and aren't waiting. Though I could truthfully say, "Godly Men Wait" and they do it right in the sight of God. Waiting changed my life and helped my marriage. I would challenge anyone to wait. It's something people rarely do either because of the love of pleasure, of freedom, hatred of discipline or the dislike of getting what they want on someone else's conditions, such as God's timing.

My Dear Sisters,

I've met many women who want to preserve their purity until marriage, yet carry the belief that men who wait do not exist. That is a double-minded belief that will never get them to exercise their faith accordingly, but more importantly something that helps them to cultivate their bad results and grow to no longer desire to wait until marriage.

What we believe, is often what we receive. If you do not believe a man will wait for you, you'll be less likely to find one. As a man who waited for my queen, I can say that women truly can set the standard. If more women stood for what they believed that they deserved and what ought to be, it would weed out the people who would not fulfill that.

'It's not coming for me' mindset, usually allows too many sisters to betray their hearts, causing them to give into what they don't want because their desire is to be wanted. Too many women hold on to men who do not have the same standards. Instead of letting them be weeded out, they try to force them to be the man for them.

When my wife said 'no more' to compromising her worth and waiting under any circumstance was her goal, she ran into me; a man with the same mindset and the same focus.

God always knows what He is doing.

Sincerely,

A Gentleman

She Isn't My Want, She's My Need

I once had a type, I wanted a Hispanic woman with a body shape like a coke bottle or an hour glass.

One who worked out with the passion of a body-builder.

One who was intelligent, sophisticated and whose breath doesn't stink on occasion, with beautiful natural long hair.

I wanted her to wear makeup as often as the holidays come around.

She had to be funny, beautiful and deeply in love with Jesus.

I wanted perfection, from an imperfect being.

While keeping these preferences, I also wanted God to be in control.

I wanted him to send me a wife and write my love story.

I sometimes prayed for and other times begged him to send me a woman who could fit those preferences.

While sitting in a church conference finding complete closure between what my ex and I had, I saw her.

She was of a lighter skin tone, appeared to be African American. She was my height, but of a bigger frame than the frame of the Hispanic women I fantasized about. She didn't look like she worked out consistently.

Her hair was long, but it was not hers but weave she purchased.

She had no makeup on, and the love of Jesus was definitely in her heart; we were at a conference where they were teaching how to live above sin and deny our wants while striving to be fully obedient to God.

I refused to acknowledge her presence for too long, experience taught me that women like her are used to being approached by packs of men. Besides, I was in the final stages of mourning the loss of my previous relationship, my heart had not yet grown legs strong enough to walk away completely.

The closer we reached the end of the conference, the more I avoided her.

She was not my type. She was loud, her voice and her laughter could be heard by the outside the walls of the church.

She carried the tomboy demeanor, which was great, but I had limited interest because that type usually carried the competitive alpha male view as well.

I had nothing against her hair, but I had my preferences and my preference was 'real only'.

The fact that she was being completely attentive while the preacher delivered God-breathed sermons; her heavy conviction and willingness to raise her hand and worship God, grabbed me.

Two days before the conference ended, I interrupted her conversation with one of my friends to start ours. An alley-oop from a buddy, I called it.

Our conversation was nothing usual. We were both writers with hearts full of poetry and the desire to please God deep in our veins.

We both longed to impact lives without wanting the publicity of it.

We had been both through hideous things, but yet to see the beauty of life.

As the conference ended, we stayed connected and our hearts became connected.

We traveled to visit each other, spent hours on the phone with one another and grew to love each other.

She became more than I desired and less like I've experienced before.

She was who I needed in my life, but did not match my want list.

I guess God gave me what I needed instead of what I thought I needed.

Preferences are great and good to have, but they can keep us from finding and experiencing love; especially if those preferences are of an unrealistic and lustful nature. My wife is not what I was looking for in a woman, many things that she is I'd bad experiences with in the past. Some things about her screamed stay away, you won't like her type. Her loudness was too much for me, her personality I believed would conflict with mine, her sense of humor I believed was the same as mine, but I could see us becoming competitive.

As a man who has grown to look for substance more than anything, I decided to not let the shallow part of me do the picking this time and went beyond the surface. Entertaining her through conversation piqued my interest and her love for God sealed it. Once we started talking, most red flags were gone, but there was more. Women I've known before to be the independent type, were full of themselves and labeled men as dogs who sniffed different women to find the ones who would give it up easily. They were too strong to let a man lead them, yet too weak to admit they wanted a man in their life.

As a single mom, I expected that to be part of her character. I do not thrive off of assumptions, but like every human being, experiences usually influenced my judgment.

Surprisingly, she was nothing like that. As I got to know her, I realized what type of woman she once was, but was no longer. She made it clear to me that she once used men for what they could do, but saw them as nothing more. The reason being, a lot of men did her wrong.

As we talked further, I grew as a result of a lot of things she explained to me in our conversations. As she grew in Christ and modeled some elders in her life, her focus changed to wanting to submit to a man who would lay down his life for her. She was no longer bitter nor felt the need to compete with a good man who entered her life. But she was cautious to let just any man lead her.

There was residue left from her doing it on her own for a long time and men consistently failing her, but she was loving and peaceful (sometimes). She was gentle and in no way interested in competing for the leadership role of the relationship, but rather in being submissive in the right biblical context. Together we were a perfect fit, her being who she truly was made me step up my game as a man to be all that she needed and all I needed to be as her man.

Men too often focus on looking at the outer appearance and basing their preferences on that. They also sometimes base things on their evaluations of a woman's character, which is heavily influenced by past experiences, instead of waiting to know her. We chase too much with our eyes, chasing our fantasies, rather than pursuing what makes a woman real and good to us.

Too many men get caught up on searching for women who fit their preference which consists of: butts, breasts, body shape and face. In doing this, they are voting out the good girl who may be perfect, but doesn't match the ideal of eye candy. It is not a trait only man carry, but some women as well. The fact is, a lot of women fall for good looks, materialistic and smooth talking men. Just like them we become victim of those preferences and end up with who we don't need but whom our lustful heart craves.

"You won't reach the next level until you move out of your comfort zone," I've heard many say, as wisdom to those who can't get desired results. I've always agreed with that and can even add, "You won't find who you need until you separate yourself from all you know." That is removing yourself from your preferences. Since those guidelines and preferences are all people know and believe there's nothing greater outside of them, it's difficult to reach that next level.

Compliments to men is what reassurance is to women. It helps nurture the good and pushes us to conquer space in the rooms we have for improvement.

Spoil Me, I Will Not Get Rotten

Though I am a man, I am made to be loved.

I am made to be appreciated and cherished.

I deeply crave affection, attention and consistency as well.

I may act as if those things have no effect on my happiness, but that is just a lie uttered by the demons who stand on women's shoulders and say, "If you stroke a man's ego, he will use that as a knife to penetrate your heart."

Believe me, if I am in love with you, your effort to make me feel that I am the best man in the world will give me enough strength to carry the world.

It will not give strength to my legs and endurance to my heart to run out of your world. That is what insecure boys who use bait to catch women do and when they feel that they have her so they proceed to catch another one.

Their egos are like unwanted children looking for approval; I do not seek validation any longer.

I am after love and to make me feel love is to encourage me to stay.

As a man I am expected to tell my woman wonderful things to help her flourish, yet nothing is said about watering my confidence and encouraging me.

What they are unaware of is that with every stroke to my ego, it paints this picture in my head that I am fulfilling my obligations to her as a man.

In a world where I can't win with women and am a loser to the average male who carries the name tag 'man' but does not live by it, it feels good to know that I am successful at something.

I do not ask for flowers, nor do I ask for an endless supply of materialism.

All I ask for is for her to spend time with me and cater to my needs as well, putting me first as I put her first, supporting me and never stop doing so.

The belief that if a woman strokes a man's ego that it will only lead to disaster, is false. Stroking a man's ego is no different than reassuring a woman that she is valuable and loved. A man's ego is not only subjected to selfishness, there are different layers to it, just as there are different layers to a male as he grows from a boy to man. An ego is no different than lust by definition, it is mainly associated with the negative, but it's not all negative.

Lust is usually tied to selfish and strong sexual desires without and that it can be damaging; yet a husband can lust after his wife, which translates into him having strong desires to please her. An ego may mostly reflect the immature, arrogant and selfish part of a man. Yet it's also pride and confidence, as well as self-esteem of a man by definition.

Stroke a *boy's* ego, it will be a disaster. Stroke a mature *man's* ego; you will get fruits of joy out of him. A man and a boy seek different things and find different things meaningful. Just as it stated in the scriptures, "When I was a child, I acted like a child." A boy wants to hear how good looking he is, how good he is in bed, how big his piece is and how strong he is physically. To him, a woman saying those things shows that she appreciates and values him. To a boy, it is proof in his mind that he did a good job of manipulating her and accomplishing his mission. When they find a girl who loves them, they pride themselves on having her locked down instead of being appreciative and treasuring her.

Children are foolish; they are ignorant of many things, so they can not enjoy things as adults do. Once a male grows, he leaves behind the boyish stages which are measured not by age, but rather growth. Stroking his ego means something completely different. As men, we want to hear that we are loved because it reminds us that the woman we are with is ours and that our heart is safe. We love security and our idea of security is the love a woman provides to us. We love hearing about our woman appreciating our sacrifices, valuing our consistency and believing in us. We want to hear positive things that our partner recognizes about us because it impacts the way we see ourselves; it boosts our confidence and influences our self-esteem.

Men do not rely solely on a woman to feel good about themselves. But it is an assurance, a reminder that we are worth something to someone. Feeling assured encourages us to continue to water our relationship because we then feel that it is in our best interest.

A woman who fails to stroke her man's ego, truly no longer has a man. It's obvious that a woman cannot keep a man who doesn't want to stay in a relationship with her. However, like every human being, a man will remove himself from an environment that makes him feel his existence is nothing special.

In many cases, it's their relationship. If a woman isn't uplifting her man, chances are she's downing him and as men, we tend to be less tolerant towards bad treatment. Stronger ones will walk away, while others will entertain attention coming from elsewhere; often leading to men falling into infidelity because they went to get their ego stroked somewhere outside of their relationship.

Men want similar things that women desire, we want to feel special, and desire to be treated as if we are valued and have life spoken into us. We want to hear things that make us feel good. Getting cocky from compliments and uplifting words is a thing of young minds looking for acceptance and validation do.

What mature men want from our women is to know that we aren't failing them and to hear from them what they appreciate about us. We do not oppose women telling us where we are lacking, but let's not forget that we, as men, want to be told what we are doing right as well. Who doesn't like a pat on the back for doing something good? Especially something not too many are doing or are doing right.

I once had a woman's heart and my only focus was to nurture it with my love.

One day, I became a fool; I grew drunk in my lust, stumbling into fool's gold. I was no longer a pirate chasing booty at night while my treasure floated away, but I became a professional model seeker whom had a woman who loved me.

I opened up my Instagram account as if it was a magazine, searching for women who left nothing for the imagination to feed my imagination. My fingers touched these women on the screen and my eyes undressed the remaining.

I did not start by cheating on her physically, but my heart was full of adulterous acts which eventually led to my fall into infidelity.

- Lustful Models

Sin's Nature

Almost every day, I am a faithful man who enjoys the company of his woman and a beautiful life with her.

On the remaining days, I am a saint who misses the pleasure of my sins.

Those are the days I do not see temptation as an enemy, but believe the lies of the snake and see it as opportunity.

My thoughts become lost, reminiscing about the fun that came with the promiscuous lifestyle.

I wonder about what I may miss out on, what experiences I will never meet because I chose to embrace the mature route of a Godly man.

It is a battle inside on those days; it's a thorn to my flesh.

My body begs me to run after the temptation rather than fleeing from it, while my spirit cries out and begs me to grab a hold of my thoughts and steer them myself.

I would be lying if I said that I do not love the look women give me at times, staring at me like the new pair of shoes they must have.

I do not spend much time entertaining their looks, but sometimes those looks stay long enough for me to wonder.

I miss the chase, the thrill I once had to acquire the heart of women however I could, the burning wants for newness.

There are times, the competitive nature in me joins in and send questions to my thoughts, such as "You think you can get her?"

"Of course, I would win her with good conversation and lots of humor," I would reply, and then proceed to shake my head upon realization of the conversation that is taking place in my head.

I used to believe that a man would keep his eyes on his woman alone and that when he found true love, he would be so lost in her beauty and character that his eyes would not look anywhere else.

On a Sunday morning I heard my pastor say, "It doesn't matter where you are in your walk with GOD, if you don't rebel against sin daily and pick up your cross daily, you can fall from any level."

Since, that sermon, it has become a reminder to me that the eyes may never be satisfied as long as they are a part of this sin-infected flesh of ours. The heart however can be bridled and steered in a direction.

Looks don't kill. It is the motive behind the heart that murders.

9 no longer believe that a man will love his woman to a point that he will never ever look at another woman. That is an unrealistic perception formed by those who still believe someone who loves you will never perform an act that will hurt you. It is a great idea, but it only exists in a perfect world. I do believe as a man grows in love more with his woman and with God, it will become easier for him to look away and close the doors on any lustful thoughts as early as possible.

Men are visual and sometimes we see things that catch our eyes. Women are beautiful to us and when we look, we have desires. I was once one of those who said, "My woman is the only woman I look at." Then I realized I was speaking something that my heart and actions disagreed with. It's easier to acknowledge that you aren't perfect and learn how to deal with your imperfections than to deny them and live under false pretenses.

Wandering eyes can help a man wander off of a good path and out of a good and fulfilling relationship, if he isn't careful.

As humans we are never satisfied. That is why rich people continue to chase money, why men with beautiful women still cheat, etcetera. Same thing goes for a man who is in love, he may have all he needs, but seeing what he doesn't have it may push him to go after it. As men, we must guard our hearts, as well as our eyes. If we let our eyes wander too much, it will lead us down the wrong route. When our eyes wander and we allow them to do as they please, we start to plant lustful seeds that will grow and allow temptation to rain on our relationships.

Looking around for me has done two things: opened my eyes to what I thought my woman lacked physically and made me thirst for newness, someone else. Many men have left a woman they have had a quality relationship with or even a marriage, for the same two reasons.

First, they start finding more things their women don't have, in comparison to what they've been looking at. Then it progresses to them thinking there is more satisfaction out there or someone out there who could make them happier; allowing them to become victims of the 80/20 rule. In doing this, they jeopardize what they have which is not perfect, but find it great to chase after what looks good and whomever has caught their attention.

The misconception we as men have is that many women we check out, we can't get or even approach. Those facts don't make our behavior as much of a threat, but we still fail to notice that when we start entertaining the idea that there's better out there or that we will find more pleasure and satisfaction out there. When we start to commit infidelity or adultery in our hearts, soon it will be manifested with the woman we can indeed get. It's like water dripping on a rock, eventually it gets through.

As a married man who has made bad choices and destroyed a couple of good things chasing what my eyes convinced me looked better, I had to learn how to practice self-control and look away. I've grown to be no longer stubborn and foolish, telling myself that it's nothing as long I don't touch.

It's not hard to find a half-naked woman in your sight anymore. There is no need to find magazines to hide and look at, you can go to the mall and see a young lady with half of her butt cheeks hanging out or her dress suffocating her flesh to reveal more than enough. You can even log on to your social network account and see anything or browse the internet for porn. I had to learn to set boundaries, to look away faster, and to cast away thoughts quickly.

Temptation is everywhere in this generation, so wisdom needs to be applied. A pretty lady is harmless, but to a committed man she can be destructive. You cannot deal with an issue or something that can create an issue if you do not choose to handle it. Wandering eyes is an issue that has to be acknowledged not only by men, but also women must recognize it as an issue too.

Without the thrill of chasing, the hunger for newness, the food for the ego, sex is nothing but moments of short lasting pleasure to many.

Without it being objectified by lust, sex wouldn't have such a great marketing campaign all across our society.

I've heard many men feel trapped with one woman because sex with one becomes boring, even men with wives.

Many of those men are slaves to lust and do not recognize that the thrill of chasing, newness and variety is behind their thinking, no different than a teenager who believes there's strength in sleeping with as many people possible because it boosts his ego.

No soul will ever see the beauty of sex until it is free from being a puppet of lust to see that without love, sex is just an exercise, an act that holds as decent because of how much it's advertised.

It's more than going to get you a new piece, more than going to perform the fantasies, more than gaining credibility because she is beautiful, more than leaving your mark so she can tell her friends that you got it.

It's more than all they've made sex out to be, it's a bonding experience with the one you want to spend the rest of your days with that will never die if one's thinking and intent is aligned with sex's original and un-perverted purpose.

Sex Objectified

Dear Mr. Porno,

I told them your secret, I told them how your videos cause my eyes to see my sisters in a different light.

Some used the pages of my book to wipe their eyes of that filth after noticing how they see women with perverted eyes.

Others used the pages to show as evidence in court making me guilty of stupidity.

I have seen women barge in the conversations and say this is not true and those looking to continue to be good friends with you yell, "Amen!"

I can say I am impressed, you and the devil have a good thing going on. He was once an angel and still masked himself as an angel of light, you used the fact that GOD created sex, and masked yourself as harmless, simply God's gift available to watch for good purposes.

Oh, you liar.

I cannot stop you when you live on so many telephone screens in this world and in a generation that sees you as crack.

But I will choose to not let my mouth be taped because of your popularity.

I have caught on to more of your secrets, the details of your lies.

I cannot believe, you indoctrinated me like this. You not only convinced me to look at more than enough women as sex objects, but as I dug deeper, I see how you deeply distorted my views of sex itself.

You told me that sex was what was on that screen. You advertised perfect butts and breasts, taught that hardcore is indeed intimacy and that sex is best without moral boundaries and that purity is a myth.

You are a liar.

You had me believing that your scripted version of sex was as real as they come, filled my heart with unreal expectations.

For the time I fought in singleness and did my best to remain friends with celibacy, you interrupted my friendship with them.

Gossiping, spewing lies in my ear.

As I waited for marriage, to have real sex with God's blessings upon it, I did not realize that you planted in my mind a false image of what's to come.

I fell victim to the things you put into my imagination. I was a bit disappointed to what the reality felt like, not because it wasn't good but because I was trying to keep up with your lies.

I searched for an experience I could only find with women who go beyond measure behind closed doors, those who want nothing attached, only some pleasure and/or money in return. Experiences that my respect for my woman will never allow me to even consider.

Sex wasn't made as a sport, it wasn't made to be without connection, it wasn't made to be a product. I stopped treating women as if they were all those things only to realize there was a residue left, that my idea of sex remained in the land of freaks and fantasies rather than the reality of love.

You are destroying the innocence of many and pushing them to crave sex in the wrong manner.

Men in love with you don't see how being in love is enough and sex daily isn't enough for them.

How unfortunate they can't find satisfaction, not because it's not alive in their relationship, but their standard of satisfaction is perverted.

You're such a liar and a manipulator, but sadly too many believe you to be a harmless puppy that they cannot live without.

Porn is not just a harmless thing. It has distorted the ways that I looked at women in my early days. Contrary to those who are on the extreme side of supporting it, it did not make me see women as completely nothing and want to sleep with them all. That reflects more on the type of person someone is. However, it did influence me to treat sex as nothing but pleasure and women I engaged with were primarily vessels of that pleasure. I saw many of them as sex objects rather than beautiful creatures worthy of my love and if I could not offer it, I should have never attempted to manipulate them for pleasure.

Porn messed me up in many ways that I could only see after I got serious about getting rid of it in my life. People who watch it don't spend enough time looking in the mirror to see what it is doing to them. Until the scales fell from my eyes, I was blind to the reality of it as well. The more my mind was purged from those toxic things, I fed my soul.

Pornography is not only damaging to a men's view of women, but to people's view on sex as well. Prior to getting married, I lived the promiscuous life. Not right up until I got married, but in my past. I was familiar with sex before, I did not consider it to live up to the hype of the what they sell. Since to me it was for the purpose of gaining cookie points or some pleasure, I never truly could enjoy the beauty of it.

During my time of practicing celibacy, there were seasons where masturbation got a hold of me and porn walked it's way back into my life. During those times, the image that porn painted in my mind that I was attempting to get rid of started once again, gaining ground in my mind little by little. My image of what sex was began to slowly be misconstrued, becoming false in that process. By the time I became married, I had quite some unrealistic expectations of sex, that are attainable only when you treat your woman as less than she is.

The anticipation I had for sex did not meet the expectation. I was not satisfied in the way I expected, though I was satisfied. Her physique did not match the women in videos, the excitement was different, and the sounds weren't as scripted and as ear pleasing. A bond and love got intimacy involved, our bodies could not outlast these videos, and we looked nothing like what I had watched. What happened was real, but the expectations were not. I had to adjust the idea of what is real and start cropping out what I thought was real.

What many fail to connect with is that porn actors are paid to act. Their body image is enhanced and modified, their performance is boosted, and there is a production and sound crew and a script. What they are having isn't just sex, it's a Hollywood version of sex. By Hollywood version I mean, it's no different than a movie with a super hero that can only exist within a movie world. Outside the screen, it's either impossible or just not real.

With porn, we feel that it's real only because it's presenting something we are familiar with, something we know without a shadow of a doubt exists and we crave. Yet, it's no different than a beautiful movie about love that some people can identify with, while you know no average love story happens like that. It plays with imaginations/fantasies and reality. I've heard countless stories of porn stars having to do enough drugs to numb themselves to do the scenes and men having to take enhancers to last and that some filming lasts longer than it seems. In addition to the changes some had to make to make their body parts more presentable.

It's a big lie. One that's hard to admit because not too many people are willing to say. The toughest part for me was me realizing that, sex cannot truly operate without a bond, it wasn't meant to be without one. When people start to treat sex as just pleasure, we start behaving like animals, without a moral compass. My fantasies of sex could not come to life when I found love because I could not treat my woman without respect, she was not a piece of meat for pleasure but another human being whom I wanted intimacy with, not just sex. There was such a discrepancy between my reality and what porn advertised as reality.

When the reality of sex settles for some men, not many are fortunate enough to take the route of trying to get in touch with what is real, because at that stage the fantasy offers more. It fits with many things in our world today. It's no different than men drooling over the bodies of models online. With expectations of skin tones, breasts, butts and other body parts manipulated by Photoshop makeup to look just like what their woman offers. Men cheat, leave their marriage, and lose themselves chasing a fantasy of sex that could not co-exist with love, intimacy and respect.

I've heard women share stories on how they give their man their all and do everything their man asked in the bedroom, yet it's still not enough for him. It is truly because when you're chasing a fantasy reality isn't enough, it can get close, but it will never be enough. I once chased those types of fantasies but I could not find it between the walls of a relationship. Relationships limited me to reality and I felt that I had to find a person willing to do anything; someone shaped like them, who acted like them and performed like them. I kept coming up empty handed and later realized it was no different than seeking a woman as perfect as Barbie.

Sex was created by God to be a beautiful thing to enjoy; it surely has been distorted today. Sex is being used to manipulate people, use them as objects, using them as entertainment or even a means to earn income. We treat it less and less like a gift, treating our bodies less and less as something of value. If I learned one thing, it is that I never noticed how something or someone influenced me, until I completely removed myself from it/them. I learned in this life that influence doesn't happen suddenly, it happens overtime.

With those lessons in mind, I always did thorough evaluations as to why I see things a certain way or why I do certain things. In the topic of sex, porn taught me far too much. As I grew, I learned new ways it affected me. It not only perverted how I looked at women, but it also perverted how I should give and receive one of the beautiful things God left for us here on earth.

I don't know how to accept compliments.

When she tells me how good of a man I am, how good of a provider I've been,

It makes me feel as if I am the best man in the world, and it encourages me.

Yet my face is empty of expression and my reactions are without life.

I hope she never grows tired of my zombie look when she uplifts me, or grows to believe that I do not appreciate them.

But I surely do, I've heard so few compliments in my life that I do not know how to take one.

I am less emotional than she is, so I don't get all giddy and blush, but I do make a mental note of what is said and use it as fuel to be better.

\-   ***Compliments***

Too Logical

Sometimes I'm too logical for my own good.

I act numb to many situations, yet my lips agree when she says, "Do you feel me?"

Well, maybe not do you feel me, but that's just to complete the metaphor.

I correct the simplest things with good intentions, but at the wrong time.

There are times when she speaks of her problems searching for comfort, and then I start to list all of the possible solutions instead of hugging her and just being a listening ear.

There are times when her ear searches for, "It's going to be okay," and I proceed to talk about how bad the reality is.

There are times her answer to me is, "God is going to make a way." Though I believe so, I spend my time trying to find the way.

On more than enough occasions she has asked me questions not seeking the truth, but instead wanting to hear something nice and I give her the hurtful truth.

I am too logical, I always have to find what is right, what is wrong and what makes sense.

Unfortunately, what makes sense sometimes isn't what's right for the moment, or what's wrong doesn't need to be treated that way.

If there is anything I have learned is that human emotions don't always agree with logic and that women don't use logic in everything.

I've learned to befriend sentimentality, it's the only thing that tells my logical mind to 'shut up', when the timing is off.

Dear ~~Future~~ Wife

Thank you for being proof that there is a woman out there for me, one who will not tally up the mistakes of my past and use them as strikes against me.

Thank you for being a woman who strives to love me despite my imperfections and for helping me perfect my heart's choice to love.

Thank you for allowing me to play my position as a man, allowing me to be the head of the household without any competition involved.

Thank you for putting up with my stubbornness, tolerating the boyish ways I am still growing out of. I know I can be hard to deal with at times but you have shown me grace and patience countless times.

I promise to be patient with you and understand that there is a trail of pain behind you that leaves memories ruling some of your thoughts or your emotions.

I will not grow angry when you make me out to be guilty for a crime of your ex-lovers. I will understand that you, the woman of my dreams, are acting out the nightmares men before gave you and you need time to wake up completely out of them.

We will grow together and I will love the ugly past out of you and build a beautiful future with no ugly moments.

I will go the extra mile to keep you happy and provide for our family.

I love you, you make me not only better but more human.

I Vow To You *(My vows to her)*

I searched for you

I searched for you in a different flesh,

in a different race,

walking through life at a different pace.

I grew tired of doing so eventually,

Tired of looking for love on my own instead of waiting on the author of love, the one who is love.

I grew tired of bringing myself self-inflicted pain, heartbreak after heartbreak ,

And when I became too tired, I traded my control for the Lord's will, His ways and His provision.

And then, He gave me you,

The best thing I can say about this trade,

 is that He knows what he's doing.

My good thing.

Your love became a flower growing through the crack of my broken heart ,

You became the moon to my dark nights,

The light of my dark days,

Oxygen to my lungs and strength to my feet,

to walk through life.

I never knew how incomplete I was without you,

I've learned that the heart and lungs are protected by the ribs and you are my ultimate rib.

I've never felt this safe loving another human being, I never craved another person this much.

Today is the day our heart syncs into one, and we become two lanes merging into one, going down the path God laid for us.

On our journey, I promise you this,

I promise to love you through the most difficult times.

I promise to love you when you're hungry and acting like Godzilla,

I promise to protect you not only physically but emotionally and spiritually.

I promise you to stay at the feet of Jesus, to continuously learn about grace, forgiveness, mercy, love and extend them to you.

I promise to be a loving example to children, so our daughters can know what a man ought to be and our sons can know what they ought to be.

I promise to love you even when our skin gets wrinkly and our hair is gray,

Well, when your skin is wrinkly... Black don't crack. You're only half.

Food may be the only thing that comes between us, but death will be the only thing that can come between and separate us.

I will love you till the end of my days, until age slows me down, until my heart beats for the last time. I don't promise an easy journey, but I know it's one that is worthwhile.

Walking into marriage for me meant taking different steps than many. Before I asked my wife to marry me, the focus was to lay all my flaws out on the table; exposing the good, bad and ugly of each other and start learning how to deal with one another. I wanted us to present our true colors and start making adjustments right away. I did not marry my wife because she's the best person in the world, but she was the best woman for me and I can see myself forgiving her for the rest of my life.

I never saw marriage as the final step; it was the beginning of a new phase of the relationship that's not supposed to end. When I said, "I do," I knew I was choosing a path that less and less are traveling for the right purpose. I was ready not for an easy journey, but one that would have many ups and downs; a roller coaster ride that I could handle as long we both held on to each other. I did not vow to her that it will be easy or that there will be no pain or tough times. But I did vow to her that I will not run during those times and that I will hold on to Jesus and hold on to her tighter when the going got tough.

I expected her to be unlovable at times. I knew she would not always be the most beautiful or the most understanding. Those things were clear to me and I wanted to make sure that they served as a great reminder. I knew if I loved her without limit that I could endure anything that came our way and I could stay motivated even when I didn't feel like it.

My love for my wife does not depend on who she is to me, but who she is. I aim to love her, the best I can without monitoring my love based on her love. Before I entered marriage, I told myself I would never keep tabs or anything of that nature. We agreed not to measure what we give to one another but to simply give. It has made such a beautiful impact.

Prior to us getting married we had already had ugly fights, shed some tears, and solved some major issues people don't handle until they are deep into their marriage. We developed that mindset that we're going to figure out things when nothing is going right and the thought of opting out of a life together, is a thought that we have started to bury already. By the time we became married, we had a 'let's solve things mentality', more than anything else. There were no new surprises, and very little was undiscussed.

Step Fatherhood

Today another man's son called me Dad.

I say another man's son simply to make it clear to you that this isn't my biological son and I am what is called a stepfather.

When I stepped into fatherhood by marrying his mother, never did I see this boy to be another man's son, but my son.

He is the fruit of his mother's loins, and his mother's heart belongs to me. Therefore, he is my fruit now.

I do not wish him to be my seed, but I consider it to be an honor to be the one who will water and nurture this tree.

I do know what it means to call another man Dad, but I do not know how it feels.

I once had the opportunity to do so, but I was too afraid because I questioned if another man even wanted me to be his son.

It was easier to say, "He is like a dad to me," than to say that he played the role my father was supposed to play.

Unfortunately, I met those father figures when I was old enough to become a father myself. Fortunately, I did meet them.

I would see in my father's eyes how much he missed me when I did see him.

A little regret hid in the back of his eyes waiting to come out as tears, tears he may have shed in my absence.

It looks like pain that only God's strength could lift off of a man's soul.

To know your decisions kept you from being what your son needs, is like carrying cancer.

Maybe not to some men, but to me, it is,

Because I've seen how it eats away the beauty of life from many fatherless men.

When I last saw him, it was the year before he died.

We were just reuniting, only to separate.

He looked like he wanted me in his life, but being incarcerated kept him away and it's clear to me now that my mother did have a part in his staying away.

I was a strong boy, a solid young man, but I'd be lying if I said his absence didn't make me doubt who I was and why I was here.

I sometimes felt like an unwanted toy that kids first want when they see it on the shelf,

They grow excited when their parents are in line waiting to pay for it. They love playing with it on the way home and on the first few days, then they don't care for it until another kid wants it.

I wonder if he was just excited when he saw my mother, happy to have her and thrilled that he would have a son until I was born, then I became unwanted.

I was young when he left and was a teenager when he came back. I've forgiven him, but those are answers I will never know.

A tear made its way down my face while writing this, the pain has left and I've forgiven him, not for the time he couldn't be there, but the time he was able and still chose not to.

The residue of what it did to me is still being removed.

I know what not having a father can do to you, and I know what having father-like men in your life can do for you.

So when I heard the word 'dad' come out of this 6-year-old's mouth,

My heart started to beat fast, this is not what I expected.

It is a testimony that I'm a good man to him, my mentor told me, but it's more of a testimony of courage for him.

He did what I couldn't do, perhaps it is because his heart is still full of innocence, but it doesn't matter. What matters is that his eyes searched for the father in me and found it.

It's like I've earned a Grammy for a role that I thought I would be auditioning for, until he becomes a man.

I realized what responsibility I have now, who I am to be to that boy and who I needed when I was a boy.

A father, an example, someone to guide him, train him up and love him.

I don't think he will ever understand how much of an honor it is to be in his life.

It's good to know I will save someone from experiencing what I experienced, having to wonder what it feels like to have a father.

The way people see it is, that I am a great step-father, but I it's hard for me to say that he is my stepson.

When I have introduced him to people, I have introduced him as my son.

And when I say that to those who know I did not get anyone pregnant yet, I quickly say, "He is my son by marriage," before the perplexed look finishes forming on their face.

It's a way of telling them that he is my wife's son first. Even that still makes me feel sick inside.

I never want him to feel that I am only playing the role of a father because I am with his mother.

I am still praying to find a way to better to say it or to not even say it at all.

I don't say it to give people a better understanding, but to clear up any misunderstandings they might have if they think I had a child out of wedlock.

Maybe they don't care, maybe it's good for them to wonder.

If there's one thing I want him to know, is that I am new to this just as he is, and I am still learning.

In today's world, it seems as if many males find it hard to accept the responsibility of being a father. I've seen countless men run to jump into bed with women and continue running when any of those women announce that they are pregnant. It's amazing when they aren't in denial or begging for an abortion; they are convincing their woman that the journey will not be one she travels alone, only to walk out of her life when the baby walks in.

I do not speak for all men, but many do pull this trick. We are living in a generation where single parenting is almost the new normal. As I was growing up, it was uncommon to see kids with both of their parents around. When both were actually around, the relationship seemed to be a bit unhealthy. I've seen many marriages that do not look like marriage, but two people co-existing with one another. It could be because I am part of a minority group, but the rate has most certainly increased in every ethnic group.

I've heard a man say, "It's unfortunate that when I find a partner, they already have a child." Many say the same with bitterness swimming in their saliva, assuming that if you find a partner with a child there will be drama that comes with it. It may sound like a bad generalization; however, it is the experience of many.

It is reality that a borderline fact to those who have experienced nothing different. I've dealt with it first hand with men who could not put their ego aside long enough to accept me into their son's life, afraid that I would replace them. Also, men sometimes use a child as a way to prevent their ex from finding something better to truly build on. They use the whole, "I don't want another man around my son," as a manipulating line to keep that woman in line.

I am still debating whether there is anything more childish than a man who doesn't care to love his woman or be a father to his child; but who grows angry when someone attempts to love her and chooses to be what he refuses to be to his own child. It's almost inhumane the way men and women use their kids to destroy any good that can come into their ex's life, but I do understand that pain is powerful and it can choke out the good out of many.

I told myself I would never date a single mother due to the trouble I ran into before. I was ready to be with a woman who comes with baggage, but a kid as a carry-on was something I could not accept for a while. I had bad luck finding a woman who would discipline their child accordingly, being mindful of the examples they are to their child or free from drama filled co-parenting.

I've always had a great connection with single mothers, due to the fact that a fair amount of them possessed a certain level of maturity that was appealing to me. The nurturer and care-giver part of them had already developed. Many of them had been on their own for a while, practicing discipline to provide a good and healthy life for themselves and for their child.

As I prayed for a wife, God had better plans than to let me limit myself because of my past experiences. He gave me, a single mother. When I met my wife, she mentioned that she had a child, from the start seeing the type of person that she was. I hinted that having a child is only a burden for men who do not intend on loving her entirely. I kept my words, I have a beautiful family.

Our son's father is not in his life due to certain circumstances; however he is as involved he can be. I have conversed with him man to man to assure to him that I will never treat his biological son as if he is any less to me. I can't find it in me to love this woman and mistreat or neglect one of the most important parts of her.

Perhaps when I was a prideful and selfish boy looking to uplift my ego, I could have possibly passed her off because of a child, but I am now a different man. I hug and kiss him on the head as if he was my first born, provide and instruct him as if he is my image. It's such an honor to be in a position to help stop a cycle of fatherless children with this boy, he may be just one child, but that is still putting a dent into the cycle.

Many young men become a spitting image of their absent father, not having a father around subconsciously teaches them that it's completely normal to have children growing up without their involvement. With this, I saw more than an opportunity to love another part of my wife, but to be an example and to help correct and build this boy. I have seen it as a chance to impact in a way different than what I do as a content creator. I saw it as me being in a position to help another person avoid the terrible routes I traveled, to learn from my mistake.

I am extremely excited about raising him in the ways of God, teaching him how to be a man by example, correcting him and showing him what loving a woman is, by treating his mother as a queen. This has been a life-changing opportunity. Years from now I can only imagine what he will add to this community, society and even the kingdom of God.

Many men become dads, but not every dad becomes a father. Fathering another man's child can be something burdensome based on perspective. I have learned to see it not as me taking on another man's responsibility or willing to accept my woman's past. This is part of my journey; God has placed me into someone's life who needs me. I am not stepfather, but a father to a great young man.

Compromising

I am like an old person who has known life to be a certain way, but does not wish to change it.

I like to go out to restaurants and eat by myself and bring home no leftovers.

I like to play Madden as early as possible and stay up late nights, writing as late as I can.

I do not like to answer to anyone because I like to go do what I want, when I want and with who I want.

I do not like to spend much time talking about problems, I simply want to solve things.

I've been blessed to have a mother who taught me everything I needed to know such as, cooking, cleaning, and washing my clothes, so I would never have to rely on a woman. Therefore, I need the house organized, dishes cleaned and arranged and my clothes washed and put up in a certain way. I am not OCD, I just like things certain ways.

I do not spend money on things I do not need. Almost every dollar is an investment to me. Therefore, I do not have a fashionable closet, I wear basketball shorts, sandals and usually a 'Gentlemenhood tee' everywhere.

I do not like to hold hands and have people in my space often. I have been fine with these routines, but those were my single ways. Ways that could hinder a relationship, without any compromising.

I cannot go out by myself anymore, nor can I go somewhere and come back without something without hearing her say, "You didn't bring me anything."

I now have to share video games with our son and have to devote some late night time to her.

I cannot get up and go wherever I please without telling her or asking if she wants to tag along.

Problems are between us now and are a lighter burden now that I have a partner. But, I must explain to her and sit and find solution with one another.

The way she cooks, does dishes and cleans doesn't always follow the way I would do it, but it gets the job done so I've learned to shut up.

Money now sometimes goes to her doing some shopping, for our son's clothes and on occasion, toys.

She buys me random shirts and pants and convinces me to wear them and dress up more often.

I am doing a lot of things I am not used to, things I never had to do.

Those things make my relationship better, the single man in me had to be replaced by the married man.

Many men cannot let go of their single ways not because they don't want to, but because compromising requires change, changes they don't know how to make or sometimes find too hard to make. There is a big transition from, "I do whatever I want" to, "I do what is needed." A transition most cannot find the strength to make and they believe that it kills their freedom. Without compromising, no relationship will thrive, and compromising is understanding that your partner will not like everything you like and want.

Dear Father (continued)

And when I found God, I figured He wasn't a mute as they paint Him to be.

How could He create the mouths of man, yet be clueless on how to talk?

Maybe He doesn't speak to them because their ears are so full of sin and their hearts so full of disobedience that they do not desire to repent.

Perhaps they never tried, living as students of tradition who made Him out to be a man of hints and nothing more.

Either way it has not been my concern, my concern has been whether I am who I am supposed to be. Or if I was living the life designed for me without letting time rob much of it.

So, I spoke to Him, I raised my voice and asked: "Who am I and where is the true me?" For this person that I am isn't it.

I've always understood that I could be nothing until I lived in the plans my creator created for me and walked into the image He made me.

My mind became full with wonder and my heart bloated with the urge to discover who I was.

I've heard from some mouths that an open line of communication with God was the fruit only a healthy relationship with Him could produce.

So I courted my savior. I devoted time to prayer, time to the scriptures, fasted and meditated in hopes He would answer me.

And when my prayers and words seemed to have been lost; floating their way somewhere in space rather than resting in the heavens, I did not stop.

I've learned that perseverance builds strength and I've seen it achieve what seemed to be impossible.

I've led my knees to become good friends with the floor and I never stopped exercising my faith whether it was working out or not.

That day came; He welcomed himself at the most unexpected time.

He whispered to me and said, "You are my son and your identity is found in me, the old you belongs in the cemetery."

I listened, those words stayed with me. I taped them to the walls of my brain though I was still short of the full understanding.

I could not see the bigger picture, but I knew the photographer.

My life became an empty canvas on which sometimes I questioned, but this time I knew the painter. I knew that Van Gogh and Picasso were only students of His and the worst amateurs in comparison to His abilities.

I learned to trust Him; I've learned to allow myself to let the understanding of the things He says to develop into my life.

Who I am and growing to be is the Spirit that dwells in me once I've humbled myself and handed Him my life.

I cannot say the man I've become is perfect, but I can say by His grace it is being perfected.

I can say that I seek His face to continue to grow into the image in which He made me.

I can say that I am a man who has a relationship with his father and daily I crave to know Him more.

I do not know where I would be if I continued my own path. I would not be anything like the man I am today. But I do know without Christ my life would be just a bunch of scrambled pieces that would never all come together.

Perhaps a few would connect but never the right ones.

It's hard to change when you don't know what to change.

It was hard for me to believe that my promiscuous ways, immaturity and irresponsible ways made me less of a man. I looked at men with morals and values and thought that it was commendable, but could never find the strength to follow their path. Instead, I became consumed by fellas on the TV screen and headphones.

Being less a man did not equate to being less human in my eyes; humans are imperfect and being a man of God also came with imperfections. So, I said, "Why not be the man I want to be?" Letting go of my ways was needed, but not wanted by me. I would fall short and continue to think that I needed to do better, but never did better. I found comfort in who I was. My lack of strength was a reason to say, "I am not perfect." Being stronger meant attempting to be perfect; the very thing no human can be. I never used the term 'only God can judge me', but I hid behind its meaning. Justifying my sinful ways, yet claiming I knew God, someone I could not possibly know if I did not stop holding hands with the devil.

Until I became a born again Christian, it seemed impossible to be good, by a standard of morality. Women are beautiful. If God didn't want me to go through them, why do I crave more than one of them? If God didn't want me to sleep with them, then why does sex exist? These are questions that I would ask myself.

Living my own way only made sense, life was about becoming who I wanted to be and I wanted a bachelor lifestyle. That included occasionally getting high, making lots of money and it didn't matter how it was acquired - any means necessary.

I was never bad by comparison to people who are criminals, but I indulged in everything that I knew better than to do. I did a lot of the things that the world normalized for young men, which I knew should not be normal. My conscience would on occasion raise its voice and say, "You can't do that. Put that down, don't smoke it, and stop drinking that. It's not numbing anything, but helping you delay your issues and live irresponsibly. Women are not toys to play with, but humans to value; stop treating them as nothing."

I was very unhappy with my life and nothing I did was making it better. The idea of becoming a man who is clean of everything, committed, married and loving God was a silly idea to me. I enjoyed the freedom of loving everything this world offers good or bad. Corruption was a way of life. Immorality was my choice and God made me free to choose. I lied, I cheated, and I manipulated people. Although my choices were not as bad as someone as extreme as Hitler, for example, they were not doing any good for me nor were my choices healing anyone.

Eventually I grew tired of myself and my lifestyle and chose to give what I considered the "right life" a chance. I decided to start following Christ after much resistance. To live right in the eyes of God became not the impossible, but something obtainable that only grace could help me reach. I would not be half the man I am without my experience of being naked of spirituality. I would not be whole without my spiritual life.

A man once asked me if I thought there could be growth in a man who is without God. I told him, "Of course, humans can grow, but internal change and more meaningful growth could not come without Him." Who I am today, a gentleman striving to be a better man to society, a better husband and a great father, would not be possible without my Christian life and values. It's what is responsible for my transformation. Without Christ, I am nothing.

They tell me life is about living your truth and being happy, yet when I choose to live for the one who is true and let my happiness rest in His hands, they tell me I am a religious nut.

They tell me to love everyone and be a good person, but when I choose to love people the way God intended me to love people, which doesn't agree with me hiding the truth and telling them there is no one good, but God is great, they mock me and say I am a hypocrite.

It's interesting that people say, "You think you're better than us," only because their hearts convict them. The way I choose to live my life is not only different, but it gets them to evaluate theirs. I've been where others have been and I have lived how they are living. A lawless lifestyle only brought me great misery.

I do not wish to save them, but hope that they meet the savior. I do not wish to shame them, but help the light of my life touch them. I do not think they are less than, but believe that they are missing out on so much more. My only desire is that my light shines brighter for Christ and every dark part of me is penetrated by the light within me.

The End

Unspoken Feelings
Of a Gentleman
III

Nagging

There are days my wife nags me for the things I am not doing, but only because she is blind to what I am doing.

We often want things done a certain way, so we neglect other possible ways that may exist.

Her reason for nagging is that I am guilty of inconsistency.

I no longer take her out on dates, buy her gifts, or spend long hours chatting about nothing.

I am either busy working, on a budget, or too tired at times.

I cannot blame her, because those things are true, but I think she is blind to my perspective of our relationship.

I would be a fool to say she doesn't deserve those things, but I would be a fool to ignore the reality of our relationship.

When we met, I was a single man established in life.

Now that I am with her, we are working on establishing ourselves, requiring more effort and hard work. A phase I was out of when I met her, but now I am starting over to establish myself as a husband and a family man.

When she came into my life, the simplest thing to do was take her out and treat her to nice things and places. For I was where I needed to be financially and I wanted her to know I was willing to provide for her.

Now that I am married to her, I do not buy her gifts as often, yet I make sure that she is provided for. I make sacrifices for us to live a good life which I think is a gift. I also picked up the habit of spending wisely and saving money which limits us to certain things.

Things she may want, but can't have until we are where we ought to be.

When we met, we spent countless hours talking about nothing, I was a single man with lots of time on my hands and I was willing to make time for my woman because I was love sick and had a hunger to know her and pursue her.

Now that we are in each other's presence for many hours every day, our talks about nothing are sometimes repeated talks. We know each other's routines and keep up with one another. I no longer foolishly disregard my schedule, acting like a teenage boy in love, but now live like a man full of responsibility. Sleep has become a necessity, my time is split between my prayer life, family, work and business.

Therefore, I am too tired to listen at times because I have to work in the morning. I am too busy to talk at times because I have to write. I cannot devote my time freely, but only with very much consideration.

But never will I grow so inconsistent that I leave our relationship laying dead behind me on my track to success.

But, I also don't want to live in the honeymoon stages. We are no longer teens with red hot love, but adults adding fuel to keep the fire of our love burning.

I've seen women who chase successful men, begging them to give them time only an unemployed boyfriend can give.

I want her to know, I'm tired because I'm providing. I don't have as much time, because I am making sacrifices. I don't spend crazily, because I am wise.

I will be more consistent, but let us get more established.

Women nagging doesn't always derive from men not doing things they need to do, sometimes it's because some women fail to see how much their man is truly doing. They fail to see things on a greater scale, which makes it hard to be grateful and easy to complain and compare.......

To be continued...